Foreword

I was fortunate enough to meet and talk with Robert Warne Wilson a number of times, in New York City, starting in 1989 with a one-on-one meeting (at my request) at his apartment at the San Remo building on Central Park West, and then here and there in the city during the following two decades. Robert Wilson, the Michelangelo of our times—certainly in the investment world, and perhaps beyond it—deigned to meet with me, a 32-year-old at first, just a layman, a friend of a friend, someone interested in the work he did. Bob was as bright and sharp a person as there is, but he also had a lot of personal generosity, I found out, and boy did he love to laugh. A person as successful as Bob had, no doubt, in some way, winning so often and for so long as an investor, been turned kindly toward the world.

Like the story of any great artist, the story of Robert Wilson's career will never get to the essence of what is ultimately an inexplicable gift. Wilson was a mythically talented stock-picker, who could routinely look at a list of twenty stocks and select the only two that were worth buying; he had "a nose for corporate death like no one else," an awed associate once said of his short-selling ability. Similarly, I have heard it said that Louis Armstrong had no idea how truly great he was; author Kurt Vonnegut said once that his books "just poured out of him"; hockey immortal Wayne Gretzky has said that in competition on the ice, "time just moved slowly for me."

Nonetheless, there is a great deal to know about Robert Wilson's career, and much to learn from it. Wilson was a man who put his talents to work with as much energy and determination, it seems to me, as Thomas Edison. Huge talent was just something to shoulder—for both men—as they went into battle to achieve as much as possible.

Killing the Market

Killing the Market

LEGENDARY INVESTOR ROBERT W. WILSON

Roemer McPhee

RMK, Inc. / New York

ISBN-13: 9781492756361
ISBN-10: 1492756369
RMK, Inc.
680 West End Avenue New York, NY 10025

For Michael,
a budding investment sharpshooter

More than anything else, I want to be rich.
Robert Wilson

The tiger in the tank is fear.
Forbes magazine, 1979

Contents

Killing the Market

Capital

People do not kill the investment markets. The investment markets kill them. A large portion of the population knows it, directly. Stocks, bonds, options, options on futures contracts, long and short positions in the commodities futures markets—just show me another way to lose money.

Like John McEnroe coming out of New York City in the 1970s, with millions of tennis players on the tennis courts all around him, all over the country, Robert W. Wilson emerged from Detroit, Michigan in the 1960s. There were investors everywhere, of course, all around him, amateur and professional, in almost every case accomplishing not much of anything (if not taking Las Vegas-style baths). Wilson received $15,000 from his mother in 1958, when he was 31 years old. It was sort of a coming-of-age present, even though he was already done with graduate school, and with two required years in the army. Wilson ran this not inconsiderable sum—perhaps $150,000 today—to the fabulous amount of $230 million, by 1986. Then, with assistance he himself sought out, he nearly quadrupled his net worth to $800 million by the year 2000. The sum of $800 million is more than 50,000 times Wilson's original stake of $15,000—from 1958. It is a capital appreciation, after taxes no less, of more than five million percent—5,000,000%. Robert Wilson did it—by himself, without partners—in about forty years.

HOW? How in hell?

It is a very important question, and this book will try hard to find, or at least get close to, an answer.

If a person looks back on Robert Wilson's uniquely accomplished career as a stock-market investor, his talent is obvious. But what was his initial, and his continuing, motivation? This is an important question that is difficult to answer. Inference is indecisive—but Wilson never talked much on the subject. I submit that from the extensive, available, indirect evidence, Wilson was as driven as President Lyndon Johnson. He just could not stand not to be somebody—not to have power. And, as much power as possible. We do know that it deeply affected Wilson as a very young man that his family occupied a "lower upper-class" socio-economic position in Detroit, Michigan, in the years surrounding World War II. He knew well, and resented the fact that his family were members of a country club near town, but that, in his words, "it was not the best." Wilson was not an athlete when very young, but as he describes it, "a loner who could be abrasive." He was bullied a bit in school by older boys, but he has also said that he was proud of out-witting them most of the time. It doesn't appear that his older brothers William and Jack gave him much of a hard time, but he did say more than once that his macho, and type-A, tyranny-of-the-trivial father so irritated him that he swore more than once that he would "buy and sell the old man one day."

When Wilson was eighteen, and a sophomore at Amherst College in Massachusetts, James Merrill, a classmate of his, and the son of Charles Merrill, founder of Merrill Lynch, took him down to New York City. Wilson was just awe-struck by the big-time city of New York. He has said that he had wanted to visit the city since he was eleven. Over the course of the weekend visit he remembers fancying himself a big New York City lawyer, or something like that. Something connected to this big-time city. Whatever he did, he fancied that it might be done there.

There are a whole lot of people determined to move and grow, and often enough, get as far away from hometown as possible. Bob Dylan shed Hibbing, Minnesota at lightning speed. Broadcaster Tom Brokaw left Yankton, South Dakota post-haste. Both Muhammad Ali and Diane Sawyer left the pleasant, low-key state of Kentucky, and never looked back. All were looking for the city where their action was centered. In many cases of super-achievers, that was and is New York.

Robert Wilson graduated from Amherst College in Massachusetts in 1946, and got a graduate degree the next year, in economics, from the University of Michigan, at Ann Arbor. Then he went to Michigan Law School, but left after two years without a degree. (This must have pleased his parents.) Casting around for work, and for a profession that suited him, he took a job at the investment house First Boston Corp. in New York, in 1949. ("The only thing I learned at First Boston was how to dress properly.") After a required two-year stint in the army, starting in 1951, Wilson returned to First Boston, but then in 1953 went home to Detroit, and there went to work again in the world of money, in the trust department of the National Bank of Detroit.

National Bank of Detroit, in its trust department, was very well run, and very well regarded. It was one of the first trust departments in the U.S. to take an interest in so-called "growth stocks." The long-standing American tradition in investing had been big, "safe," mature businesses, that paid reliable dividends to shareholders, who generally depended on them. A growth stock, on the other hand, was a younger and smaller public company that would not pay out much income, but instead try to grow capital, through growth in sales and earnings, and thus stock price. These growth stocks were riskier than, say, IBM and General Motors and General Electric, but among their advantages was much better tax treatment. Dividend income in the U.S. was taxed as high as 90% at the time, and capital gains only 25%. Clearly, Wall Street and direct investing beckoned Wilson. In the late 1950s he said that he had failed at everything else, including law school at the University of Michigan, and that he would try investing, as a last hope. The irony here could not be larger. Well trained by National Bank of Detroit, his appetite for investing whetted, to say the least, in 1958 Wilson left Detroit and went to work in money-center New York City, first at closed-end investment fund General American Investors, and then, from 1962-68, at investment house A.G. Becker & Co.

Wilson, married just two years, to Marilyn, received the very significant sum of $15,000 from his mother, in 1958. He was 31 years old. He took it with him to New York, adding it to his own investing account, and the two Wilsons moved into an apartment in Brooklyn, near the Brooklyn Bridge. His inheritance of $15,000 was no insignificant sum: probably $150,000 in today's money. Receiving it was a seminal moment in Wilson's life, as he has said. He understood it to be such, at the time. It was no modest amount, as it would be considered today. It was a major piece of money, a grub-stake for any would-be investor; an amount to be taken seriously, at least. No trifle. But what to do?

Robert Wilson had learned a very hard investing lesson in 1956, two years earlier, when he was 29, and it might be the most important lesson that he ever learned, and the one that set him on the path to greatness. He took all of the stake he had at the time, about $20,000 (from working since 1949), and put it into two very fine stocks: IBM, and Houston Lighting & Power. Unfortunately (though not surprisingly), Wilson was leveraged to the hilt. He jammed these two positions on on full margin—at the time, the 75% maximum that was allowable. In other words, Wilson bought $80,000 worth of these two stocks, with his $20,000 in cash.

Well, there was a stock crash in 1956. Wilson's account fell 25%, wiping out his equity completely. His broker sold him out, since there was no money left in the account, and Wilson went home and cried on his new wife's knee. IBM and Houston L&P recovered quickly in price, and went on to new highs, for months and then years.

Wilson was livid—and chagrined. He was a Depression baby, one of those people growing up in the 1930s who could sometimes feel, and for the rest of his life, that the world is about to come to an end. One of those people who could be pessimistic in spite of best efforts and desires to be the opposite. ("I'm from Detroit. That's where I learned the market can go down 90%," he said to me once.) Wilson's father had taken a shellacking in bank stocks in the Depression (the worst stocks to have owned, it turned out), and only his mother and her decent-sized inheritance had saved the Wilson family. Robert Wilson vowed never to operate in the stock market again, without protection: protection from the market.

What is absolutely key here, and completely fascinating for any student of Wilson's career and its grand success, is how he defined "protection." Wilson apparently did not think for a minute that what had got him, what had ruined him in 1956, was borrowing lots of money. The problem was that he was not short as well as long stocks, simultaneously—to protect against broad market movements. That was the problem, indeed. ("Selling short": borrowing shares of stock from a broker, and then selling them in the marketplace, for cash. The repurchase and return of the shares, at some point, any point, in the future, is required. A profit is made if the stock price goes down.) No doubt Wilson did a pro-forma study here. If he had been short $40,000 of stock at the same time he bought $40,000 worth of IBM and Houston L&P, he would have been just fine! The market crash of '56 would have knocked down his smaller long position, and boosted the value of his equivalent short position, at the same time! Moreover, he would not have been shaken out of two great stocks, but gone on to the grand capital gains that they made for their other shareholders in the ensuing months and years. No, it wasn't the borrowing that was the problem. Wilson knew it in his bones. It was the hedging, the protection of short positions vs. long positions, held at the same time, that had been missing from his investing. It would never be so again. Never. It could almost be said that the hedge-fund industry itself was born right in this moment.

The Tiger in the Tank Is Fear

"You would not believe some of the shit I've owned."
WILSON

Robert Wilson had been "straightened out" in a major way in 1956, but it is better than a guess that he sensed his extraordinary investing abilities at this point in his life, and was at least willing to put his own toe in the water again, in the markets. Quickly. To try to make his own money, directly, for himself, and in a big way. This time as a genuine hedge-fund operator, who was not going to let the broad market and its vagaries knock him for any kind of serious loop.

With $15,000 from his mother, and a new family, Wilson tried the stock market again, in 1958. What is very soon startling about him is his renewed and even increased aggressiveness. He was more aggressive now than he had been in 1956! And what is truly mysterious is the portfolio genius that he displayed as he designed his approach to stock-market investing: his policies on the selection of individual stock positions, both sold short and bought long, and the portfolio policies, and the heavy borrowing that he did, that would allow him to make more money, faster, than anyone else in the business, and shoot to the moon and beyond.

There is no argument from anyone who knew him that Robert Wilson was an impatient man, and it became apparent early that that was never more true than when it came to money. Wilson wanted to make as much as he could in the markets, and as fast as possible. But how, exactly? How, above and beyond the obvious need for the protection and insurance of a hedged portfolio? There had to be more involved than just good defense; Wilson knew it. What Wilson came up with was the idea of the explosive stock, the wild and crazy stock. The stock that was held by the fearful, or the greedy, or both, and thus had the potential for a big price move. The individual stock that had publicity and public attention, and was drenched in human emotion. Stock-market investing is an entirely human process, after all. Hedged fully, Robert Wilson didn't care if a stock went up or down, so long as it moved. Driven by fear, or greed, or, ideally, both. Otherwise, what is the point?

Going further, and getting at the essence of Robert Wilson's investing career, is not easy. We have to use the power of rhetoric, it seems to me—and particularly, metaphor.

At some point in the middle 1950s, to early 1960s—from the evidence—Robert Wilson's natural genius told him that he had to operate a methamphetamine lab, so to speak, in order to get as rich as he possibly could, in the U.S. stock market, and with as little delay as possible. Wilson could have done a thousand other things in the investment business, of course, and far more pedestrian, but to maximize his potential as a stock-market investor, which is what he clearly wanted to do from the outset, he had to run the equivalent of a methamphetamine lab.

What is methamphetamine? It is well known today, unfortunately. A very powerful drug that can be created privately, in a home-grown lab, at very low cost, and sold for a great deal of money and profit. But—"meth" has the ability at any time to blow up in your face, maiming you seriously, and for good. In other words, "meth" is potentially lucrative, and always very dangerous.

In 1958 and 1960 and 1963, etc., as Robert Wilson grew more and more observant and mature as a player in the U.S. stock market, he clearly came across the aforementioned central idea of the wild and crazy stock. The wild and crazy stock, truth be told, would be at the very center of Robert Wilson's crusade for wealth. Like President Lyndon Johnson, Bob Wilson, Brooklyn, New York investor, wanted to MOVE. And as fast as possible. What, Wilson might have asked at the time, is the point of a T. Rowe Price conventional growth-stock investment, or some predictable dividend payer like General Electric or IBM or Procter & Gamble? Or some predictable stock of any kind? Those stocks aren't going to take their shareholders anywhere fast, and they don't. What Robert Wilson determined was that he was going to center his investing on the scary business-equity share, the stock that scared the hell out of people—even him—because it was impossible to know what was going to happen next. But something—a move up or down in price—was going to happen. That was for sure. And probably a dramatic one, a violent one. Robert Wilson founded his investing on the stock that scared you in the nighttime, and made you fearful to take a look at its price the next morning.

O.K., you have built yourself a methamphetamine lab. One thing is certain—something is going to happen. Something big. There are going to be stock-price moves, as it were, and big ones. How do you protect yourself from the inevitable explosions? How do you protect yourself from getting killed? How do you protect yourself from things blowing up on you—from 50% stock-price collapses all over the board?

Portfolio Genius: Heavy Diversification, Full Hedging

"When the stock market crashes, why then,
'good men go down together.' HA!"
WILSON, 1990

To stay alive, let alone succeed, in the investment game, arguably the toughest business in the world, Robert Wilson figured it out that you run 200 or 250 separate methamphetamine experiments at any one time—all sealed off from one another. No recourse, one to another, anywhere. There were going to be disasters, and big blow-ups in his portfolio, but with the wild and crazy stock as the central item, there were going to be huge financial gains, as well. And Robert Wilson, with a large faith in his already proven abilities as a stock picker, knew that his average portfolio results could be huge.

Robert Wilson once told financial reporter John Train that he would be "scared silly if my long position were only ten of my stocks." (This was in 1979.) At the time, Wilson owned seventy long positions. John Train continued on in his article that this was the most useful thing he had ever heard Wilson say.

In 1962, well employed in New York at investment house A.G. Becker & Co., analyst and salesman Robert Wilson underwent the test of his young career. It was an unexpected, but very valuable, test of the investing and operating procedures he had established in the late 1950s, after his personal financial debacle in 1956. What would happen? Would things hold together now? Would the seasoning Wilson had experienced at ages 29 and 30 be good stuff, or false—deadly nonsense? Would his hedge-fund concept hold together? Theory didn't count for much, here. Or ever. Experience was everything.

The U.S. stock market broke badly in 1962. Worse than it had in 1956. It took a huge, general hit to the downside. Wilson's fully hedged private portfolio actually got knocked down in value quite a bit—but, as expected, not as badly as the Dow Jones Industrial Average, or the Standard and Poor's average of stock prices. (Wilson's long positions had gone down more than his short positions had gone up in price.) At the low point, the stock market in 1962 was down an average of 40%, and Wilson's portfolio at the same time was down something close to 30%. He had begun 1962 with a net worth and portfolio value of $300,000. He was taken down about 30% at the low, to $210,000, but then recovered with the market, and ended 1962 at $300,000—exactly unchanged. Wilson was not upset, he was delighted, as he looked things over. He was a hedger, an aggressive hedger, and he was right to be one. Nobody and nothing could bust him. It brings a bit of a chill to hear what he told his wife Marilyn at this point: "Now I know that I can get rich. Now it is just a matter of getting rich."

It is important to note that the only consistent thing among Robert Wilson's stock-market investments was that he thought, at least, that they could all move in price. Move up in price if he owned them, or move down in price if he had sold them short (creating an obligation to buy stock shares back later). Beyond this common characteristic, there were several different themes in Wilson's stock portfolio, as he himself has said. Wilson had great regard for business innovation. Innovation was a natural, automatic competitive advantage, and could cause a big advance in stock price as the particular business captured revenues and profits other companies were not capturing.

Wilson also said many times that he was looking every day for "new wave" businesses. Again, a natural competitive advantage over other businesses (and whole business sectors). A recent example of new wave is the internet stock, which appeared on the scene in the 1990s. If Robert Wilson had been actively managing money then, there is no doubt he would have been all over the situation, and owned dozens of these stocks.

Wilson was also on the lookout for surprises. Key developments in a business that were not appreciated or understood by the investment community, at least not right away, and could cause real changes in the company's fortunes, and position, and stock price.

The "wild and crazy" stock mentioned earlier was not by any means always a small business, or a marginally capitalized business. It was just capable of wild stock-price movements. These movements could and would occur, Robert Wilson judged, for many different reasons, first and foremost those several just mentioned.

The short side of the market, short-selling stocks, and thereby simultaneously creating credit balances, and obligations to buy all shares back (returning them) in the future, at whatever price available, also interested Wilson very much. Down was the other direction, the second direction, in which stocks could and often did move, after all. It was potential price movement, and that meant money changing hands. Money changing hands from someone else, to Robert Wilson (most of the time, as it turned out).

In 1968, Wilson formally went out on his own as an investor, forming the hedge fund Wilson & Associates in New York City. He had been wildly successful at A.G. Becker, in the 1960s, trading in his own account, and he began with the princely net worth and grub-stake of $7.4 million. Throughout the 1970s, he became famous in the financial press as a bear, a short-seller of stocks. But he did not become famous because he was doing something arcane, or super-negative. He became famous because he was right. He was properly aligned with a negative marketplace. And being right made him rich. Wilson remarked at one point, "I had God-like success on the short side in the 1970s. I shorted about a thousand stocks, and maybe five went up."

Robert Wilson first became famous, as a short-seller, because that's where the action was. That's where the money was made on Wall Street, at least in the economically rough, inflationary years of the 1970s. But short-selling is overrated and overexposed in the press, as Wilson would be the first to point out. It is a simple matter of mathematics. A stock sold short can only return 100% to the seller: a sale of a stock at $100, that subsequently goes to $0, and out of existence, yields the short-seller a profit of $100. The stock that is purchased at $100, on the other hand, has no limit on potential profits, and may ascend to $1,000 and $2,000 and beyond. In other words, there is a floor on price movement down, but no ceiling on price movement up. Ultimately, in his career, Robert Wilson made far more money owning stocks than selling them short. Short-selling was insurance and portfolio hedging first, and a profit-center second. It was a way to let those lucrative long positions keep growing, without getting margin calls from a bad market. Even in the 1970s, Wilson at any given time always had more money in stocks he owned than in stocks he had sold short. But—it is important to try to harvest all fruit.

All of Robert Wilson's money came from the U.S. stock market. Yes, there are many other stock markets around the world, but the home market was plenty big enough to play in, he had obviously decided very early in his career. Wilson, for all his famous aggressiveness as an investor (taking enormous individual stock positions), had an extraordinary sensitivity to the market, as well. He was very sensitive to its themes, its moods, its changing moods, its dreams and its fears. This was the very complex animal that fed Wilson, and as anyone who looks at Wilson's very famous and public career can tell, he developed every sensitivity he could, to extract as much treasure from the market as possible.

Wilson said something quite marvelous at one point, long ago: "I know absolutely everything. But I am willing to change my mind." Unlike millions of hard-headed, insistent investors out there, insisting on this idea or that, and treading water or losing money, Wilson worked very hard to understand the complexities of the U.S. stock market, was always determined to be aligned with it properly, and was as flexible as a willow, and could change his mind in a minute. As brave and tough as Wilson could get while trading stocks, and as rich as he became, the stock market was always his master. Beyond his talent, this attitude might be the single most important clue to his grand success as a professional money man.

Another crucial example of Robert Wilson's obeisance to the U.S. stock market is the way in which he timed his holdings of investments. He liked to call himself a "long-term trader," but the first issue was always, of course, making as much money as possible. If a stock investment could run forever, like the wind, very well described by Alice Schroeder in her biography of investor Warren Buffett (entitled "The Snowball"), Wilson would own the thing forever, as well. A great growth stock makes an investor's life simple. It pays new capital gains all the time, as the stock price appreciates, it doesn't have to be sold, and the taxman can thus be kept at bay forever. If you don't close out the investment position, there are no taxes, local, state, or federal, ever.

Geometric Progression— What They Don't Understand

"[To be an investor], money has to be the most important thing in the world to you."
WILSON

"T. Rowe Price is a big name, but how much money does he have? Not all that much!"
WILSON

Robert Wilson once said, "A profit on a little bit of money is only a little bit of money, but what people don't understand is that this process can compound before long into an enormous amount of money." In other words, if you make 30% on $10,000, you have $13,000 a year later. Staying with such an investment position, and thus avoiding capital-gains taxes, the next year a 30% gain will produce a total of $16,900. In the following year, the same gain will produce a total of $21,970 for the overall portfolio. It is not easy to make 30%

per year in the market, but it can be done, and here in a simple example is the miracle of compound capital growth. In three years, at 30% annual appreciation, an investor will have 120% more money than he or she started with.

Wilson was actually able to compound his net worth, his portfolio of investments, at the breathtaking annual rate of 35%, after taxes of course, between 1963 and 1977. His average compound growth rate over his entire investing career, after taxes, was a very formidable 28%. It produced the following, select set of results:

Year	Net Worth
1958	$15,000
1960	$195,000
1962	$300,000
1966	$1 million
1968	$7.4 million
1971	$12.4 million
1972	$21 million
1977	$42 million
1980	$81 million
1982	$110 million
1983	$173 million
1984	$154 million
1985	$197 million
1986	$230 million

Annual tax-planning is of course crucial, to protect a compound growth rate. Any cash that is paid out in taxes from a portfolio is not only gone, but reinvestment gains are also lost. If the portfolio growing at 30% is going to be out $5,000 because of taxes, it will also be out the $1,500 that would have been made the following year, and the $1,950 that would have been made the year after that, etc., etc. Ad infinitum. It is a bit of a financial tragedy. Thus tax-planning is very important to a successful investor, and Robert Wilson did a great deal of it.

Leverage Artist, Extraordinaire

"The last time the United States was debt-free was 1835."
RAND PAUL

As an investor, Robert Wilson always borrowed prodigious amounts of money, and it is a very big, though not very well known, part of his wildly successful career story. Without a lot of borrowing, without heavy leverage, Wilson would not have compounded his net capital, his net worth, at the rate he did, and he would have ended up with far less than the net $230 million he had when he quit the business in 1986, and handed the management of his money over to about twenty hand-picked professional managers. Wilson's career is a premier example of the successful use of other people's money.

A crucial point about Wilson's investing is that he believed that risk was centered in a lack of hedging; a lack of protection from hedged investments; a portfolio where stocks were owned and not also sold short, in a big percentage of overall portfolio value. Wilson evidently did not see borrowing large sums and percentages of money, in a hedged portfolio, as a big risk, and evidently, he was correct. It is one of the truly profound insights into the investment business ever achieved, and ever demonstrated. It is an insight that cannot be proved theoretically; it has to be demonstrated, and proved beyond any statistical doubt. Wilson demonstrated it, over thirty years of steady investment work. If borrowing were as dangerous as many people think it is, it would have eliminated

Wilson and his money and his career at some point between the late 1950s and the late 1980s. He was always heavily leveraged, and yet he always survived, and survived very well.

Wilson's stock-picking was usually first-rate, on both the long and short sides of the market. That fact has long been established. Let us imagine for a moment that Wilson's investment portfolio is a bit like a fine sphere, a globe; a miniature earth. It is near-perfect in shape, and it is beautiful and orderly. Now imagine that this pretty little world is five times larger than it once was. So, vastly larger. None of its grace and order are lost; it appears the same as the small sphere, in that everything inside and outside remains proportionate. It looks the same and operates the same as the small globe; nothing is out of balance and nothing is inferior in appearance. It is just a whole lot larger. This is what Robert Wilson did by investing with lots and lots of borrowed money. Without changing the nature or the quality of his work, he put it on a grand scale, and took on (tax-deductible) debt-service expense. The nature and the structure of his investing did not change with leverage, but everything was much bigger and the money, and the profits flowing to Wilson, were much bigger than they would otherwise have been.

There is a great old saying about debt: it requires you to get up in the morning, and go to work. The reference is to debt service, the cost of debt, the interest on debt that always must be paid, month after month. This old saying is true, but in the case of Robert Wilson it must be shaded a little bit. Wilson had to pay margin interest to the various stock brokers who lent him money to buy stocks; he had to pay money to other (overseas) commercial banks that he himself brought into the process; and he received considerable interest payments from the credit balances he created by initiating his many large short positions in the stock market. With his borrowed money, and his short credit balances, Wilson was paying interest twice, and getting paid interest once.

Everybody, and every corporation, every borrower, has to cover debt service. In Wilson's case, that meant that he had to bring in more capital gains than he paid out in interest (obviously he never thought that this was a big deal, in part because interest payments on investments are tax-deductible, and capital gains may very often be shielded from taxes). But the above is not the real issue with a borrower like Wilson. The real issue is just how much, just what percentage, you borrow against equity. Wilson, throughout his career, wanted a very aggressive 80% leverage on his portfolio. In other words, for every $100 of equity, Wilson wanted (and in fact got) $400 in borrowed money to work with, as well.

A final key point about investing with borrowed money is that you have to believe in your ability to beat the market, short-term and long-term. Clearly, Wilson had great professional self-confidence. There is no point to getting aggressive about, and expanding, a bad project, or a bad investment program, of any kind. There is a very good argument for expanding, leveraging, and boosting a winning project. This is true not just in investing but in all of industry. Bankers are always looking to lend to winning industries, to expand and speed up operations and results. The only real question, as mentioned above, is just how much leverage to use.

80% leverage, 80% debt, is far more than the Federal Reserve Board, which sets the margin rules for all U.S. investors, or the New York Stock Exchange, or any other U.S. stock exchange, has ever allowed. And here is where things get interesting. Robert Wilson was determined to get way past the normal 50% "initial margin" allowed on a stock investment, or the 30% "maintenance margin" that has been set by the New York Stock Exchange, and has long been an industry-wide convention. What did he do? He went overseas, to overseas bankers, to borrow money against his investment equity—first in Mexico, and then in Switzerland. He did not deceive the NYSE, but he certainly did not feed them this information, either. When Wilson got to the New York brokerage firm A.G. Becker, in 1962, at what he (and many others) calls the start of the "go-go" years on Wall Street, he met Max Lowy, a colorful bank chairman down in Mexico, who heard Wilson out and decided to set up a credit account for him, tied directly and exclusively to his personal stock portfolio in the States. Wilson regularly, and always, let Lowy and his people know his (audited) net worth, his collateral, so to speak, and then he continued with his work as an investor—on a much-expanded basis.

Wilson has said many times that his years at A.G. Becker, 1962-68, were the years when he got rich. His portfolio of stocks grew steadily larger in number, and much larger in overall value. In 1966, he became a millionaire. ("The only office title I am interested in around here is millionaire.") By 1969, he was worth more than $7 million. Wilson wanted 80% leverage in his investing, at all times, which in the case of $7 million in equity meant $28 million in total borrowings. He could only get about half that amount from his domestic stock brokers, under U.S. law. Evidently as Wilson requested $10 million and more from overseas, this proved to be too much for the Mexicans. Wilson was so success-ful in the stock market that he needed bigger leverage than banker Max Lowy was willing to provide, and the two parted ways amicably late in the 1960s. Now Wilson started borrowing money from—who else—the Swiss, principally through the flagship bank Credit Suisse, out of Zurich. Wilson soon developed the habit of traveling to Switzerland three times a year, to see his new bankers. They got to know him well, and that didn't hurt anything. His big and expanding net worth made the bankers feel safe, and they were happy for Wilson to turn on this big money spigot that they provided, when he needed it. It was very much like the common revolving line of credit used by corporations. As usual, as with the Mexican lenders, the Swiss required of Wilson an annual, audited statement of overall net worth. And of course, Wilson's bank collateral, his net worth, was always nicely liquid—just cash and marketable securities.

Getting maximum exposure to the stock market for the smallest (prudent) amount of equity possessed was not, and is not, entirely a matter of cash. In the late 1950s, working at the closed-end investment fund General American Investors in New York, Robert Wilson looked with envy at the member firms of the New York Stock Exchange—for one particular reason. They did not have to put up any margin capital, in cash or securities, to maintain a short position. Non-members were subject to the 50% initial-margin, and 30% maintenance-margin rules, as usual. If Wilson could duck this requirement on short positions somehow, he could put on a lot more short and long positions without putting up any more cash or securities to back things up. With zero margin required for short-selling, he could expand his overall exposure to stocks in general, long and short. And short-selling was, of course, vitally important to Wilson. More than a way to make money, it was crucial insurance against down-drafts or worse, in the market. Wilson viewed a big short position, hedging what was owned, as nothing less than the thing that would keep him in the game, no matter what.

Wilson looked into turning himself into an NYSE member, as a sole pro-prietor. The compliance rules, from the NYSE and the Securities and Exchange Commission, were daunting, and discouraged him immediately. The NYSE did not want its members using advantageous margin rules for their own accounts; only floor traders were allowed to sell short without margin, because, in the NYSE's theory at least, it provided liquidity to the market. Money managers operating for themselves were not allowed to take advantage, just for them-selves, of NYSE membership.

Wilson gave up on this intriguing idea. He would just have to tap the Swiss for more money, and pay a little more in debt service. And then deduct, write off, all the debt service at tax time.

Robert Wilson's insistence on heavy investment leverage did quite a bit, at one point, to shape the course of his career. Early in 1968, the higher-ups at A.G. Becker, the managing partner and others, who had known about Wilson's borrowing from Swiss banks for quite some time, told him that the practice made them uneasy; increasingly uneasy. It was clearly something that the Securities and Exchange Commission and the New York Stock Exchange would not like, if they found out about it; it was clearly a violation, in spirit if not in letter, of the margin limits that all American stock exchanges, and the Federal Reserve Board, set for U.S. investors, to keep leverage in the home stock markets limited. Robert Wilson, in characteristic fashion, said that he took "a full half-second" to come up with a response. He would go out on his own; he would leave A.G. Becker, so that he could continue to borrow margin money from overseas. His job was one thing; his capital and his method of operation were quite another, and far more important, and could not be messed with or disturbed. He felt that it was essential to his work. Wilson was worth more than $7 million at the time, and there was no question that he would be worth far less if he had not been borrowing money from the Mexicans and the Swiss since the time he first got to A.G. Becker, in the early 1960s. Wilson and the firm parted ways amicably; everybody in the firm enjoyed, and to varying degrees depended on, sharing investment ideas with one another. They hoped to continue to do so.

In 1968, Wilson formed Wilson & Associates, in New York City. He started to manage money for a few family members, and for some wealthy friends in Boston. The new firm began work with $3.5 million in capital. Wilson continued to manage his own money, of course, but he kept it separate, in large part because he knew he could not operate as aggressively with other people's money as he could and did with his own. As an example: overseas borrowing would not be part of the new firm's activity.

There was a major stock-market top in December, 1968, and then things generally started to head south. Even for hedge funds. Wilson's clients didn't lose as much money as the general public around them did, but a lot of these people became discouraged. They were not professional investors, of course. While Wilson's own net worth increased to $8.3 million in 1969, at the same time he watched his Wilson & Associates clients start to withdraw money from the firm.

1970 was a very rough year for stocks. There was a 40% break to the downside, into a low in September. The story of the year is what a lot of people might guess that it was. Wilson and his own money went into the hole, along with that of his clients. At the deep, scary September low, Wilson & Associates' performance was down 35% for the year. Most of Wilson's clients left right at this low—they withdrew their funds at absolutely the worst moment. The firm's capital, with withdrawals, and to a lesser extent because of losses, dropped to just $350,000 at one point. This was just ten percent of its starting value, from two years earlier. Then it recovered, on an annual-performance basis, to about break-even, by year-end 1970. In just three months! So did Robert Wilson and his own money. Wilson was not impressed with his clients' behavior, or sense of market timing, and he determined to put no emphasis on work for clients in the future. It was not what he was about, and it was not where the money was. He remarked, "It's too bad they left when they did. They were at the start of a 1,000% gain!" By the end of 1971, Wilson himself was worth $12.4 million. By the end of 1972, he was worth $21 million. Sayonara, everybody. There was, in fact, only one Robert Wilson.

The Individual Stock Positions, Short and Long

"It's been a quiet life. The market has provided the excitement."
WILSON

"We all try. You succeed."
RICK BLAINE TO VICTOR LASZLO, IN "CASABLANCA,"
THE GREAT FILM FROM 1942.

With approximately 200 stock positions in place in his investment accounts at any one time, short and long, and, therefore, hedged against broad market movements, Robert Wilson could take great chances with an individual investment position. He had wrapped himself in the asbestos raincoat of diversification, the protection that always comes with large numbers. So why not swing for the fences with an individual bet? Meaning, not just get involved with a wild and crazy stock, but also in a very large position? That he did. The downside could be steep, but the upside might well be fabulous.

There are few things more powerful than a good example. Robert Wilson was involved with so many thousands of stock positions over thirty years that it seems that a good way to understand his portfolio and his portfolio work is to look at individual investments. In the list that follows, for quick reference, the capital letters L and S indicate whether Wilson owned the particular stock (long), or had sold it short.

Datapoint [L]
Innovation, and Years of Tax-free Money-making

Datapoint Corp. was for a very long time a part of the engine room of Robert Wilson's investment portfolio, as it was for all of its owners. It was a stock owned (not sold short), and for years it went up in price as the business greatly expanded. Essentially, Datapoint led the way, and took the very first steps, toward moving the computer out of a large room, owned by a government agency or a corporation, and onto an individual's desktop. At the center of this effort, at first, was Datapoint's invention of better and quieter computer terminals, using television screens; and ultimately, the invention of the central-processing-unit on a single integrated circuit—the computer on a chip, the computer inside—the world-shaking microprocessor. It has been said, and it is true, that the microprocessor in many ways has made modern life possible.

Year after year in the 1970s, Datapoint's business seemed to keep rising, like a sunflower on a hot day; its compound growth ultimately turned it into a Fortune 500 company, in 1980. Datapoint was one of the great "snowball" rides that investor Warren Buffett likes to talk about: the stock investment that just keeps rolling on its own, picking up more and more snow (sales and profits), getting bigger and bigger all the time. Owning a stock like Datapoint in the 1970s was and is the holy grail of investing: no work to be done, no taxes to be paid, new capital coming in all the time—it is the gift that keeps on giving. It is like owning and holding onto IBM Corp. in 1946, at the dawn of the computer age; or Walmart Stores, when it first was a public company in 1970.

The great semi-conductor maker Intel Corp. usually gets all the credit, but Datapoint was right there at the invention of the microprocessor, in 1969. The founders of Datapoint actually brought Robert Noyce, Intel chairman at the time, into conversations about the microprocessor that they had conceived and designed, at least on paper—looking for technical and financial help. In any event, Datapoint went public in the fall of 1969, and within a year its stock price had risen from $8 to $45.

Robert Wilson famously watched even the tiniest public offerings of stock (all of them a matter of public record), and throughout his career he read the business press voraciously. Datapoint caught his eye very early after its initial public offering of common stock, in 1969, because of the fabulous, revolutionary microprocessor. Datapoint was founded on innovation, so completely that very early on it attracted the attention of industrial giants like Intel, Texas Instruments, and TRW, all interested in potential partnerships with the young company. Its first public offering of stock was for a lonely $4 million. Robert Wilson loaded up on Datapoint stock soon after and never looked back, and never sold any shares on the precipitous way up. The ride lasted more than a dozen years, from 1969 to 1982, when the very large company ran into some serious trouble. At the top, Wilson had made fourteen times his money in Datapoint. A 1,300% gain. He had compounded his original investment many, many times over—tax-free.

Bowmar Instrument, mid-1970s [S]
Mr. Toad's Wild Ride

Bowmar Instrument in the early 1970s was a Robert Wilson stock. It had been the first and was then still the second-largest manufacturer of hand-held calculators in America. The pocket calculator since about 1973 had been the center of a popular craze, in the U.S., and also in Japan. The American public (the largest market) was fascinated by the novel product, and also dived into the common stock, as investors. The stock price soon went beyond any reasonable value—and then far beyond it. There were no real barriers to entry into the pocket-calculator business, and giant competitors lurked in the wings. There was a lack of vertical integration at Bowmar, as well (meaning that Bowmar did not control the supplies of components it needed to make its products). A price war in the calculator business seemed inevitable to Robert Wilson—and Bowmar was a high-priced company in a very vulnerable position. He asked at the time, "What is a calculator, but a couple of semi-conductors in a metal box, with some buttons?"

He started selling Bowmar Instrument short at a fairly high price, around $20 per share. He thought he had been patient with the big rally in the stock. But, no matter. The market didn't see things Wilson's way, and the stock price kept rising. First to $25, and then to $30. Wilson was down 50% on his overall position. Unlike almost every other short-seller in the investment business, this price rise inspired him to sell more. ("If I sell short and the stock doesn't go against me at least 20%, I start to think I've done something wrong.") Wilson, firm in his original business conviction, kept selling short Bowmar. Still, the stock kept rising. Then still higher, and higher. Wilson just kept expanding his short position—thousands and thousands more shares of stock sold short. The (international) hand-held calculator craze had become, frankly, in 1974 and beyond, bigger than anyone, amateur or professional, had ever imagined it could be. And still, Wilson hung on to his position. Bowmar stock hit $40 per share. $42. $44. Wilson was down more than 80% on his position, and his money, even though he had been selling short all the way up. Thank God for all those other investment positions he held—many dozens of prospering shorts, dozens and dozens of profitable longs. There was plenty of portfolio equity, and plenty of margin money, to stare down the myriad screw-heads and neophytes out there, who were herding together and pumping up Bowmar Instrument stock day after day. ("I have an icy resolve never to cover a short position.")

Bowmar stock leveled off above $40. Then, one day, it started to look wobbly. Bowmar Instrument, rightly concerned about its lack of control over its basic component, the semiconductor, the basic component of the hand-held calculator, decided it would put $6 million into a new semiconductor plant of its very own. It delivered a big press release to this effect, and it was met almost simultaneously with the announcement by giant Texas Instruments Corp. that it, too, would be entering the hand-held calculator business. Texas Instruments was among the largest semiconductor manufacturers in the world, and entry into the calculator business was an obvious move, and would be easy, and very lucrative. Essentially, Texas Instruments (and other big semiconductor makers, who soon followed suit) had the goods to get into and stay in the fast-growing calculator business—and Bowmar Instrument did not. Particularly not with the arrival of giant competition.

Bowmar stock began a nose-dive. A good business had suddenly turned lousy, and looked like it was going to stay that way. Bowmar stock fell for two years, and went way below all of Robert Wilson's original short-sale prices. In 1976, the company filed for bankruptcy. Wilson covered—bought in—his entire short position at an average price of $2 ½. He had made another small, seven-figure fortune in the market—by being right, and by hanging tough.

His most famous comment about Bowmar at the time: "That was a rough one!"

And there are two comments about the short side that Wilson made later, which are still well remembered on Wall Street: "To be a short-seller you have to be a masochist, and then try to make money later on." And, "You sell short at a nice high price, and then the market keeps pumping up the stock after you've sold it."

Lockheed Aircraft Corp. [L]
Betting on People

Lockheed Aircraft Corp. was from its earliest days a builder of weapons systems and aircraft for the U.S. military. It had great success in World War Two, selling fighter planes to the U.S. government and the Air Force. Seeking to broaden its business in the 1960s, it put its toe in the water as a builder of airliners for the civilian-transport market—namely, the big, wide-body, three-engine, L-1011 airliner. This plane was meant from the outset to compete with the very successful, rival Boeing 747, known as the first "jumbo jet." Lockheed committed to building 500 L-1011s, known as Tri-Stars, but big problems with the project developed very quickly. The costs of the L-1011 turned out to be much higher than forecast; and Lockheed faced a serious bottleneck when its sole engine supplier, Rolls-Royce in England, could not deliver power-plants on time. The L-1011 business was very expensive, a big part of overall costs even for Lockheed Aircraft Corp., and senior management announced in 1981 that Lockheed would cut the L-1011 project in half—from 500 jumbo airliners, to 250. The last order for the plane, due in 1984, was the last one the company would build and deliver.

Lockheed had always been an innovative, creative, very high-earning supplier of complex weapons systems, and some fighter jets, to the U.S. military. In fact, the leader in the field. Corporate management sensed, and the point was obvious, that a civilian jet and a civilian program were not its business. Sales were half what had been hoped, and profits were less than nil. Actually, Lockheed lost plenty of money on the L-1011 project, and in 1981 they said they were getting rid of it.

Robert Wilson entered this situation and took a long position near $27 per share. Lockheed Aircraft was worth owning—the number-one seller and earner, supplying the U.S. military. Even with the L-1011 project in place. Getting rid of this big project was like a perfectly good aircraft remembering to pull its flaps up, while in cruise flight. An obvious mid-course correction to be made, to an otherwise perfectly good aircraft (and business)—and then the future was going to be just roses. At the time, noting the impending closure of the L-1011 project, Robert Wilson said that "the stock, at scarcely over twice earnings, will soar."

Great students of the U.S. stock market, like James Finucane, out of Chicago and Colorado, have made the key observation that stocks will trade up and down, to very unreasonable levels, because of quarterly earnings reports. While earnings might swing wildly, due to temporary circumstances that are positive and negative, the great indicator of the health of a business—revenues and sales—is almost always a far more stable statistic. The fact that it is not well heeded presents great opportunity for investors. Lockheed Aircraft Corp., in 1981, had a phony earnings problem, because of the L-1011 airliner, and a very strong and stable, nay expanding business enterprise, overall. The company had the most interesting and most sophisticated weapons systems on offer anywhere, and sales to the military were strong and growing fast. Management cured its earnings problem quickly and easily by getting out of the civilian-airliner business permanently, and returning to its terrific core business. Lockheed stock went nuts, to the upside, more than tripling in price. Robert Wilson, of course, was on board, and had been for months.

Baldwin-United [S]
Late to the Game, and Winning Anyway

What is traditionally very hard for amateur investors to understand is that it is never too late to buy into a winning stock and business, and never too late to sell, or sell short, a loser. In fact, professional short-sellers often prefer to wait until the end of a company becomes near and clear, so that their sales of stock are definitely going to make money. It doesn't matter if a business going bankrupt is sold at $2 or $40; the destination is still a price-per-share of—nil.

Baldwin-United, a big insurance company based in Cincinnati, Ohio, with many subsidiaries, centered in Indiana and Arkansas, wondered in the late 1970s, as so many insurance companies did, what to do with all of its money. Insurance premiums of every description rolled in all day long, and the investment wing of the insurance business, traditionally a huge money-maker, started to get the concerted attention of top executives at Baldwin. They decided, in 1979 and in the following years, to plunge head-long into the annuities business. Interest rates were high and could only continue to go up, correct? It could be nothing but lucrative for cash-rich Baldwin-United.

The company sold $3.4 billion worth of annuities to its insurance policy-holders, and to other members of the public, over four years or so. The company guaranteed a first-year interest payment of 14%, followed by fixed payments for the many contract years following, at nothing less than 6-8%.

What the top executives at Baldwin-United did was make a very large bet on interest rates, essentially—and one that the company did not need to make. Like the average trader in high-interest bonds—any member of the general public—Baldwin was incautious, and dumb as a rock, at the bottom of the bond market. They had also succumbed to the common gambling instinct. They sold the bond market short, and massively so. Trying to make big money in the interest-rate game, assuming that a strong trend of rising interest rates would last forever, Baldwin-United ended up buying the top in U.S. interest rates. In other words, it sold $3.4 billion worth of annuities at rock-bottom, with all their attendant, long-term fixed costs. Unawares, the company had contracted to tie a giant albatross around its neck. As interest rates declined, Baldwin's own fixed-income invest-ment income declined, but obligations on annuities, of course, did not. The emo-tional top executives at Baldwin (just gamblers?) wrecked their whole business.

All kinds of well regarded losers, in business and out, decided at the low to sell short the U.S. bond market, at the end of the 1970s and early into the next decade. Entire banks went bust by selling the bond market short—playing the interest-rate game, and ending up dead wrong. Bank executives had far too much power, in many cases, to gamble with bank assets. Super-trader Richard Dennis, out of Chicago and the bond-futures pits, as smart as Baldwin-United and others were dumb, became convinced in the spring of 1981 that U.S. inter-est rates, particularly 30-year long-bond rates, had peaked. He purchased 2,000 bond futures contracts, an enormous position, that would move $2 million in value, up or down, for every full point in the price of the 30-year Treasury bond. Before the year was out, he had made about $25 million, from a dramatic decline in bond interest rates, and a corresponding increase in bond prices.

Baldwin-United kept selling its annuities to the public all the way into 1983. Well after the general interest-rate top. Very soon the whole company became strangled by its contracted, gigantic, regular interest payments, and other enor-mous capital losses in the fixed-income markets. Robert Wilson took note—the story became very big very fast—and, confessing to the press that he had been "very obtuse when it was higher," Wilson shorted Baldwin-United stock heavily around $3 per share, and ended up pocketing every dollar he was able to transact for. ("Always kick a dog when he's down," he would say about short-selling.) There was no turning back Baldwin-United. Its fate was sealed. It was one of those ideal short sales: bankruptcy and liquidation were certain. Just a matter of mathematics. Selling short at a low price, Wilson pocketed every dollar that he had been able to raise through his short sales. Eventually he purchased a significant number of common shares back "against the box," to protect himself against capital-gains taxes. But apparently he didn't press this matter as far as he could have. Wilson had a marvelous, oft-repeated saying: "Be a gentleman, and pay some taxes."

Compaq Computer Corp. [L]
The Brass Ring

Robert Wilson missed Microsoft Corp., which went public in 1986, but since the late 1970s he had been focusing on the very grand minicomputer, and personal-computer, revolution. The movement of computer power away from government and corporations exclusively, and then, incredibly, on to individuals everywhere. There was a ton of money in this massive shifting of the ziggurat, this platinum investors' vault, this grand new personal computer ("p.c.") industry, and the right investment judgments held the keys to fortunes. Microsoft Corp. had achieved a substantial lock on the personal-computer software market, by signing contracts with the behemoth IBM Corp., and still retaining ownership of its operating-system software; but there were many ways to approach the personal-computer gold-rush—software included. Personal-computer hardware had not been turned into a commodity, at the time (the commodity that it is today), and Compaq Computer out of Houston, Texas decided to make the best-built and best-engineered personal computer on the market. The company built some of the first IBM-compatible "clones," machines that could run the same operating-system and applications software as the IBM p.c., and these Compaq machines were built well, by engineers with an average fifteen years' experience. Compaq signed a partnership agreement with Intel Corp., virtually the owner of the integrated-circuit microprocessor, and gained an enormous market advantage by featuring first, over and over again, the latest-generation Intel chip for the personal computer.

As a marketer, Compaq determined very early that it would sell its personal computers through dealer networks—and not through direct sales efforts, a la

Dell Computer (founded in 1984 in nearby Austin, Texas). This policy allowed dealers a wide range of pricing options, with their attendant marketing strategies (low price, high volume—or the opposite). Compaq decided not to compete too aggressively on price, as the many other start-up clone manufacturers were doing, and the marketplace ended up voting strongly in its favor, responding to the better functionality, construction, portability, and reliability of its personal computers.

Compaq's three founders were all senior engineers and managers, who had departed the giant semi-conductor maker Texas Instruments in 1981, agreeing that the big company was making serious strategic business mistakes. What the three friends saw in the burgeoning personal-computer business was a lot of manufacturers treating the p.c. like a commodity. It was not. It was very difficult to manufacture properly and well, and Compaq moved in with a clear effort to seize the potential competitive advantage that it saw. Compaq paid up for very experienced engineers and designers, quality-control professionals, and even, astute marketers. It became known as the maker of the Cadillac of personal computers, even though its prices were never much out of line with the IBM p.c. itself. A great deal of its market appeal, apparently, was public hunger for an alternative, any good alternative, to the dominant IBM p.c. Compaq out-engineered and out-manufactured its competitors into the late 1980s, when other companies really did begin to catch up to Compaq's production standards. Then, the commodification of the p.c. business truly began, and price wars became very frequent. But Compaq Computer had grown huge, hitting $1 billion in sales in 1987, five years after its founding, by diving into the p.c. gold rush early but correctly, with correct strategy, and plenty of intelligent advance planning.

Compaq Computer went public in 1983, and Robert Wilson took a heavy long position in the stock (this is all the detail he would give the press). He always seemed able to spot an innovator early. And this innovator meant particularly large capital gains: Compaq was eventually purchased, twenty years after its founding, by the Hewlett-Packard Corporation, for $25 billion.

The Real-Estate Investment Trusts, 1960s [S]
Cooking the Books

In the last year of his administration, in 1960, President Dwight Eisenhower signed "the REITs" into law, and into being. The idea had come out of the U.S.

Congress. Real estate is of course a very large, crucial investment area, and always has been, and the Eisenhower administration's idea here was to obviate the problems of scale and let the American public get involved in diversified, commercial real-estate investing. The typical REIT was publicly held, in the form of liquid securities—liquid, marketable shares—and was organized much as a mutual fund was for stock-market investing. The underlying assets held by a REIT would commonly include office and apartment buildings, shopping centers, hospitals, warehouses, and even undeveloped timberlands. The new idea was a hit with almost everyone, but the new REIT "industry" soon had a lot of predictable shakedown problems. One of the biggest was in its accounting practices. Real estate investments, in general, are governed by many complicated tax laws; there are many deductions allowed, and very complex depreciation and income-recognition rules to follow.

The American public came to adore the high-yield REIT investment, income-heavy with those big dividend payouts, and in the mid-1960s Robert Wilson became convinced that REIT income was being manipulated and overstated, to attract investment, and that the situation was masked by clever financing of federally required dividend payouts to shareholders of at least 90% of taxable income. Inflation did not really get going (and get out of control) in the U.S. until the arrival of President Lyndon and his endlessly expensive Vietnam War, and REIT investments were supported in their early years more by popular enthusiasm than upward, inflationary pressures on real-estate prices. This situation allowed accounting scandals in the REIT industry, which started appearing in droves after 1965, to take hold of, and plunge, REIT prices. Wilson made as much as 50% on some of his short positions. An investor can always get a very good move in a short position if the investment goes from popular to pariah. Emotions run very high, and for a very long while.

Burroughs Corporation, 1960s [L]

Burroughs Corp. and Compaq Computer were two Wilson investments held twenty years apart, in the 1960s and the 1980s, but it is important to mention Burroughs Corp. because in Wilson's case the two companies share the same theme. Burroughs was an old-line business-machine maker that in the 1960s became one of the nine largest computer companies in the United States. It was, in fact, second (a distant second) to the behemoth IBM Corp. In the 1960s, "computer company" meant a designer and builder of big mainframe computers, for industry and government.

Burroughs, number-two by a mile, nonetheless tried, like IBM, to offer a full product line to its customers: not just mainframe machines, but printers, disk drives, tape drives, even computer paper and printer ribbons.

IBM had led and had been feasting on the computer business, in its various developing forms, since 1946. It was always the industry leader—until it lost control of the personal-computer business in the 1980s. Robert Wilson was fascinated by different ways to get at the riches of the giant industry, and always by looking past and underneath the famous and popular (and richly priced) IBM. In the followers' group of eight, early in the '60s, he noticed great innovation and competitiveness at Burroughs Corp. IBM could not capture every crumb falling off the table from its huge market, and a great deal of money flowed Burroughs' way because it was a full-line company that was also an original designer of mainframe computers. Burroughs came up with three separate mainframe "architectures" in the '60s, each designed to support a different, popular mainframe language (an established, existing software code): ALGOL, COBOL, and FORTRAN. This market approach was logical, and also unique, and it was just what customers wanted. Burroughs made a ton of money with its specialized big machines, and for years in the business gave IBM a serious run for its money.

Wilson's investment in Compaq Computer in the early 1980s is a lot like the Burroughs investment, and not at all just because IBM was involved in each case. One of Wilson's dictums is that in a gold rush, in a huge new market, look for the lesser knowns, who are innovative and clever and hard-working, because they have to be to survive. These lesser lights have far less stock-market exposure than the leader(s), and their necessary efforts and creativity can often lead them not just to survive, but to prosper greatly. And particularly in a rich business like computers.

Pizza Time Theater [S]
What a Disaster

"No amount of investment money can start a trend, or stop a trend."

Stock-trader's maxim

Hubris is probably the central piece of the story of the downfall of flash-in-the pan Pizza Time Theater, Inc., early in the 1980s. Entrepreneur Nolan Bushnell had founded the wildly successful Atari Corp. in 1972. Atari Corp. was a true original: with its video ping-pong game, and a "ball" moving left to right, back and forth on a video screen, it was the very first video game. Nobody could imagine, not even Nolan Bushnell, how enormous this business, this video-game industry, would soon become. Bushnell sold Atari to chairman Steve Ross and Warner Communications in 1976, for about $30 million, and then in 1978, believing in what he must have thought was a continuous Midas touch, he purchased cost-heavy, barely profitable entertainment-operator Pizza-Time Theater from Warner Communications. He merged it with Chuck E. Cheese, Inc., his own company, founded the year before, in 1977. This whole thing was a plan to build the video-game market, one way or another, single-handedly, if necessary. The sense behind it was thin to none. Market trends start and stop on their own, and are not respecters of persons.

Bushnell's Pizza Time Theater, Inc. went public in 1981. The idea was to expand the market for video games in general, to a very major new demographic, and "population": children. These video games, these electronic wonders, had been very popular amusement for adults, mainly, in pool halls and bars, and similar spots. Nolan Bushnell wanted to bring in the children, en masse, and make a fortune off their millions of fresh quarters dropped into vast numbers of freshly built video-game slots, as the kids ate pizza and watched Pizza-Time Theater's cheap animatronics (moving, electronic characters, like a poor man's Disney World). After a completely surprising, huge decline in the video-game business, beginning in 1983, Nolan Bushnell really started digging himself a hole. He didn't consider strategic changes; he pressed on with his original business plan. He seemed to think that he, the video-game king, the original, could not fail at an expansion effort, in spite of major warnings from the market. He thought that he could single-handedly revive the video-game business by continuing to try to create more markets for it.

After 1983, and the video-game "crash," Bushnell's high-cost version of his original, lean success, Atari Corp., was overwhelmed by costs and expenses, and soon filed for bankruptcy, in 1984. Initially, Bushnell certainly seemed to think that he could re-create the old, grand success of Atari Corp. in the 1970s—by putting his head in the sand and spending money on a losing game. In 1983, all Robert Wilson saw was Bushnell spending a fortune to stay afloat with Pizza Time Theater, now a bad business. Bushnell was spending hand over fist, self-deluded, getting swallowed in a whirlpool, throwing good money after bad.

"[The business has turned lousy] and they aren't earning any money, and I think it's a disaster," Wilson told Barron's weekly newspaper. Wilson was heavily short Pizza Time Theater after the video-game "crash" of 1983, and he spent nothing to cover his short position in the stock. It went to zero.

The brilliant Robert Prechter, an investment-newsletter writer of high repute, said once that "the best thing you can do in bad times is to fold up and shrink down, and in that way protect yourself." In other words, like Robert Wilson, always be properly aligned with the marketplace. Go with the flow, which you cannot control. Don't ever "fight the tape," as they say on Wall Street.

Tandy Corporation [L]
The Harder I Work, the Luckier I Get

In the dark days of 1974 in America, into and through President Nixon's resignation in August, and the super low in the stock market at the end of the year, Robert Wilson started buying the common stock of Tandy Corp. This company had long been a very clever mail-order retailer of craft and hobby merchandise, and leather goods, and it had started planting small retail stores across the U.S., as well. What Wilson particularly liked about Tandy Corp. was that it had owned Radio Shack, Inc. since 1963. This meant high-margin consumer electronics—audio and video devices and ham radios, etc.—pumped through a big and rapidly expanding distribution system. Tandy Corp. expanded into Europe and Australia as early as 1973, and in five years of blinding growth after 1969, it expanded its U.S. store count from 132 to 269.

Robert Wilson could not know it, of course, but Tandy Corp. in 1977 legged into and helped start the personal-computer revolution. It was an enormous piece of good luck for investors, of course. Tandy Corp. had its own manufacturing assets, and began offering one of the first fully assembled micro-computers (not a kit), along with Apple Computer Corp. and Commodore International, Inc. In 1977 Tandy came out with the TRS-80 model, and in 1980 with a color-computer version of that machine. It had 300 stores to move the brand-new micros out to the public, at a time when there were almost no other computer retail stores in the U.S. The prominent InfoWorld magazine called Radio Shack "the dominant supplier of small computers."

There are many ways to get involved in a big revolution, and in the case of the advent of the personal computer, retailers of these machines were going to do just fine. In the "p.c." gold rush, there was plenty of money to be made by everybody, and especially in the earliest years. Tandy Corp. was not only the dominant U.S. retailer for quite a while; it had the great foresight to start manufacturing the micro-computer machines as well, for its own account.

Tandy Corp. was a very fine investment that did much better than Robert Wilson thought it would. But, he always tried to bet on people, and Tandy management was first-rate, and with fine judgment they jumped into the personal-computer business right at its birth. In fact, they were among the founders of this great new industry. Wilson went along for the ride, and it helped him reach a net worth of $26 million by the end of 1975.

Denny's Restaurants [L]
Nothing Wrong with a Piggy-Back Ride

As an investor, Robert Wilson wouldn't touch famous market leaders, generally. They were famous, that was their problem, and their price-earnings multiples were pumped up as a result. But in any successful and expanding industry, he always scoured the second and third ranks for investment ideas. These smaller companies were part of a very good game, and they might do very well indeed, because nobody paid much attention to them initially. There was a lot more room to expand, as a stock and a business. This is a lot of the story behind Wilson's investments in Burroughs Corp. and Compaq Computer: these companies, in a bit of a shadow, nevertheless feasted off the giant business led by IBM Corp. As they grew, they gained respect, and higher "p-e" multiples in the marketplace.

Wilson and the whole world saw the arrival of McDonald's Corp. and fast food, in the early 1960s particularly. McDonald's Corp. went public in 1965, in a huge and very successful offering of common stock. Wilson had long admired the innovative Denny's, which had gone public in 1961, and he could see also that McDonald's Corp. was going to expand the fast-food business greatly, for everybody involved. Denny's founders had changed it from a donut shop to a coffee shop, and then started serving breakfast food, mainly, and it was one of the first 'round-the-clock, 24-hour operations of its kind. Denny's planted new stores aggressively, and it did wonderfully in the 1960s particularly. It reached a nationwide store-count of more than 1,000 restaurants, in all fifty states, by 1981. The common stock expanded faster than the business itself, largely because the price-earnings multiple expanded as well, with increasing public awareness of the company.

American Airlines [L]
Very Predatory

Historically, the airline business has never been much of an investment. Costs are heavy, profit margins are thin, and competition is generally fierce. And the price of oil hangs around your neck, unpredictably, like some kind of godawful albatross. Robert Crandall, erstwhile chairman of American Airlines, as savvy an executive as the industry has had, once said that "if the Wright Brothers were alive today, Wilbur would have to lay off Orv." He also observed that his own company was a good one to manage—but not to invest in.

The airline business is traditionally a zero-sum game, because of its lack of growth, and low barriers to entry by new competitors. If an airline company is going to prosper, it is going to have to take its prosperity out of another company's hide.

Robert Wilson understood that innovation takes many forms. The classic form, the invention of a completely new product that catches everyone else by surprise, and makes a fortune, is only one form. In the case of American Airlines, in the early 1980s, Wilson noticed true innovation, as one competitor learned how to attack and defeat others. An innovative ability to win market share from other airlines, and take for itself a larger slice of the same old pie. American was big enough to cut its costs below those of its competitors, by using a "hub and spoke" system for delivering passengers to their destinations. (This ingenious system was pioneered by Federal Express Corp. years earlier—see section below.) A regional airline can only deliver a passenger point-to-point, but a large, national carrier like American can and did deliver passengers from one point to any other point in the country, by sending them through a central "hub." In American Airlines' case, that hub was Dallas, Texas. Chairman Crandall also developed the first frequent-flyer system in the industry, known as SABRE; and he used many different financial incentives and discounts on tickets, to cement customer loyalty.

The airline business in the early 1980s was stagnant, but American Airlines under Robert Crandall was on the move, chewing up competitors and improbably making lots of new money. The airline was like a pickerel, in a pond full of vulnerable trout. It became what an airline almost never is: a great investment. Wilson loaded up on the stock. He always had his hand on the sell switch, because this was the airline business, but he was not rash about making a fast buck and getting out.

Federal Express Corp. [L]
20/20 Vision

Robert Wilson had been fond of the airline business since 1964, when with the arrival of the major innovation of the jet engine, he had made ten times his money in Northwest Airlines, for himself and his clients at A.G. Becker, in New York. But he did not usually have a lot of investments in the industry. There were really none to make. Industry innovations were few and far between, and the airline business was generally competitive and low-margin, and, therefore, lousy.

At the beginning of the 1970s, the hard-charging, visionary, no-nonsense Fred Smith arrived on the scene. He was a former Marine Corps pilot, and he was convinced that high technology, particularly in the computer world, required fast delivery of high-value parts and equipment of all kinds. The only way to do this, Smith reasoned, was through air transport. And, some kind of new cargo airline.

The great advantage here, Robert Wilson and other investors realized immediately, was that the air-cargo business in the United States was hidebound. There was lots of regulation, and to get, say, a computer chip from one end of the country to the other, that required inter-line agreements among air carriers.

Fred Smith raised more venture-capital money for his new Federal Express Corp. than had ever been raised before in the U.S., for a start-up business. While still a private company, in the first years of the 1970s, the company was down $25 million at one point—"just skimming the tree-tops," as Fred Smith said. That was the financial low point, and as everyone knows, the business went straight through the roof from then on. Federal Express went public in 1973, and Robert Wilson took a large position. He could see what was nothing less than the amazing and very surprising reality of a new airline, enjoying huge barriers to entry by potential competitors.

The other thing that Wilson appreciated about Federal Express was its ingenious use of a "hub-and-spoke" delivery system. In the nature of its business Federal Express had to be a national airline from day one, so it immediately established a single central city, a central city-hub, for itself. (Not at first, but eventually, this was Memphis, Tennessee.) There are enormous efficiencies and cost savings to be achieved by transporting people and cargo through a national system of "hub" cities—if the operation is big enough to accomplish it. (In other words, not point-to-point, like a regional carrier, but point to any other point in the entire system, through centralization.) From its very first day of operations, with twenty French Dassault Falcon jets, Federal Express Corp. was a national airline, and a national delivery system. Not just a regional one. It had to be. But this also allowed it to operate "hub-and-spoke" from the beginning—big enough to be very efficient and very cost-effective.

National Video [S]
The Fever Breaks

One of the great innovations in consumer electronics was the color television set, which arrived on the scene in the U.S. around 1965. National Video was a Chicago-based manufacturer of television tubes. With tremendous sudden excitement across the U.S., and Japan, and elsewhere, over the prospect of moving from black-and-white to color TV sets, National Video immediately had far more orders for color television tubes than it could fill. A severe shortage of color tubes developed. National Video, with few competitors, working at full capacity, and trying to expand capacity, watched its stock price soar, from approximately $4, to more than $40. Robert Wilson decided to pay close attention to the big U.S. manufacturers of TV sets—Magnavox, Zenith, Motorola, etc.—to try to gauge when the wild frenzy would end; when the bottleneck, the logjam would break up. He declared to his close friend and fellow investor Richard Gilder, "As soon as I hear that…anyone can get [color TV tubes], I am going to sell short National Video, and in great strength."

Wilson went to a luncheon to hear the president of Magnavox, and the president of Magnavox said exactly that. Wilson started selling short National Video near $40, and he kept selling as the stock rose into the low 50s. Wilson at one point was down on this short investment by 25-30%, but he held on to the position. He had plenty of equity elsewhere, in plenty of other short and long stock positions. If he believed in an investment, he could and would ride out adverse price swings.

National Video eventually returned to a stock price of $4—exactly where it had been before the mania developed over color television. It looked like nothing had happened—but lots and lots of money had changed hands among investors, both on the way up, and on the way back down.

Northwest Airlines, 1964 [L]
The Arrival of the Jet Engine

Robert Wilson always said that he hand-picked the stocks he wanted to own, and on the other hand sold stocks short more or less as a "group." In other words, corporate trouble and/or death was to Wilson more of a general concept, affecting whole business sectors; while a bet on business prosperity was, for him at least, usually centered on a specific business, a specific "star" company.

Wilson also said, however, that his big investment in Northwest Airlines, in 1964, which turned out to be a 1,000% winner, was as close to a group or "macro" long investment as any he ever made. It was a bit of an exception, in other words. The broad idea was the arrival of the jet engine, and jet-engine technology, as the new standard in civilian air transportation. It would make civilian-airline costs much lower, and revenues much higher, per "seat-mile," in industry parlance. And particularly on long-haul routes, which were a Northwest Airlines specialty at the time and later. Northwest was the largest U.S. trans-Pacific air carrier after World War II, with a major hub in Tokyo, Japan. It started flying the three-engine Boeing 727 airliner late in 1964, and fresh revenues and profits just poured into the company. Basically, Northwest was doing an awful lot of high-profit long-haul business, of both people and freight, and the arrival of the jet engine then expanded good profit margins dramatically. This was the era before deregulation of the industry (in 1978), so fares went down only gradually as costs collapsed. Robert Wilson could see it coming. The jet engine was a technological innovation of major-league importance to the airline business. It was a double-play, in his thinking, since airline revenues went up and costs down at the same time. This made a stock like Northwest Airlines an even better investment than Boeing, which made the jet airliner, or jet-engine manufacturers themselves.

Postscript: As soon as Wilson saw competition growing significantly for Northwest Airlines, and jet travel becoming something approaching common, he liquidated his long position immediately, in a single day. The sale was so startling that apparently only half his clients at A.G. Becker followed suit, in spite of his recommendation. They had prospered mightily, and grown very content, owning this stock. Wilson had no illusions about the business they were all in. It was about making money, and then protecting it. Always protect capital; and never fall in love with any stock. A nickname arrived, and stuck: "U-Turn Wilson."

K-Mart [L]

Robert Wilson was never involved with Walmart Stores, Inc., but he was well aware of the ongoing post-war boom in American consumer retailing. Sam

Walton, founder of Walmart, had sensed as early as the mid-1950s that there was an immense, neglected consumer market out in American small towns, and also in the suburbs, which were growing leaps and bounds because of the automobile (and some urban flight).

Walton decided to start a chain of discount department stores, bringing "urban" goods to local and rural markets, and at the lowest prices he could afford. Interestingly, the S.S. Kresge Corporation was right behind him. Kresge was a long-time five-and-dime retailer equally enamored of the high-volume, discount retailing business model, and it opened the first K-Mart store in 1962 in Garden City, Michigan—four months before the first Walmart store opened.

The first high-volume discount retailer in America was certainly E.J. Korvettes, founded in New York City in 1948. This company was a huge hit, and it suggested to very good strategic thinkers at S.S. Kresge, and entrepreneurs like Sam Walton, and others, that the idea would work even better if this retail opportunity were brought to the vast underserved populations of suburban and rural America. Thus, with K-Mart and Walmart and Sears, and others, the big-box store was born.

The business model was first-rate, as everyone now knows, and K-Mart took off right from the get-go. In the 1970s, it was so successful that it put a number of competing retailers out of business. Until the end of 1990, it was the second-largest retailer in America, behind Sears.

A key reason why Wilson bought heavily into K-Mart was simply that it was available—started by S.S. Kresge (which would change its name to K-Mart), a public company that had existed since World War I. While K-Mart and Walmart got going in 1962, Walmart did not go public until 1970. K-Mart was the first public stock of its kind, and it was as pure a play on big-box retailing as Walmart would be.

Horn & Hardart [S]
Short Orders Aplenty

In 1984, Robert Wilson trained his guns on the famous old Automat food vendor, Horn & Hardart. Lots and lots of great old businesses, unable to turn the corners in fast-changing times, go down like giant Mammoths, with lions chewing at them and jumping up and climbing all over them. Horn & Hardart in the early 1980s was a company just swamped by competition that had sprouted up all over the place, from fast-food businesses of every kind. Its large Automat business was low-cost, but it also ran waitress-service restaurants, cafeterias, and bakery shops. The coin-operated Automat itself had gone out of fashion years earlier; for a long time the American public had much preferred dealing over-the-counter in a restaurant for its fast food, or with an operator in a drive-through sales window. Horn & Hardart bought a fast-food business of its own in 1981, Bojangles' Famous Chicken, but it was far from enough to turn things around.

McDonald's Corp., the seminal fast-food business, went public in the mid-1960s. Its growth was so dramatic that competitors spawned quickly, and a whole new industry arrived, at first on the American scene. Americans in particular fundamentally altered the way they consumed food, locally and while traveling on the road. Saving time was more important than anyone but McDonald's, and company leader Ray Kroc, apparently had realized. If food could suddenly be had quickly and cheaply, an individual person's day could be altered, in very positive ways. Time could be freed up for many other things.

Horn and Hardart in the 1970s and '80s was a stolid and high-cost business that simply did not have the ability to make fast and fundamental changes to its operations. And those were the only things that could have saved it from fast food—this shifting of the ground underfoot. Robert Wilson, waiting until quite late in the game, into the early 1980s, had probably decided to bide his time until this particular business situation was irretrievable and irremediable. In other words, he finally concluded in 1984 that Horn & Hardart was definitely going down and out—down into bankruptcy. This is the kind of short sale that many professional short-sellers take. They wait for certain business doom, with a stock price still alive in the public market, because at that point every share you sell, and every dollar you raise by selling stock, is going straight into your bank account. The end price is going to be zero. There will be no higher cost at which to cover your short sale, and get out of your investment position. If you sell short at $10, you make 100% on your sale. If you sell at $4, you make 100% on your sale. And, afterward, there might even be a way to avoid taxes.

Jordache Jeans [L, and S]
Roman Candle to Whack-a-Mole

Robert Wilson always kept his eye on retailers. He knew what Maryland money-manager Charles Allmon often observed, that a retailer can make a ton of money if it catches, let alone dominates, a new consumer trend. And a retailer can also flare up for a while, and then die. Fashion trends were, to say the least, no exception to this rule. A fashion retailer was almost always going to have volatile business results—just the thing Wilson loved to see.

The three Nakash brothers out of New York, founders of Jordache Jeans, Inc. in 1969, had always been interested in the denim business in Europe. Jeans were much more fashion-forward there than in the U.S.; form-fitting, generally, and thus higher priced. The brothers decided in the late 1970s to make this kind of denim clothing for the U.S. market. It would provide true differentiation for them, and they sensed that a high-end jeans market, a "designer jeans" market, could develop in the States.

In 1979 they ran a very aggressive ad campaign, in print and on television, financed with one-third of total company revenues. Retail sales took off. The Nakash brothers boosted Jordache's ad spending dramatically in 1980. Soon Jordache started licensing its brand aggressively as well, developing as much as $300 million in annual sales, at the wholesale level. They got to as high as one hundred separate licensees, late in the 1980s. There was a great deal of excitement and volatility in Jordache stock, something that Robert Wilson loved. He bought in heavily, and suspected as well that somewhere down the road, things might flame out, as consumer trends so often did, and that the stock could make a lot of money for a short-seller, as well.

Early in 1982, Wilson dove into Salant Corp. as well ("plunged," the Wall Street Journal called it). Salant was a mid- to high-market menswear apparel company out of New York, with several strong brand names, well established in the marketplace. Salant was a way for Wilson to keep legging into the consumer craze in jeans, and also, gain a bit of diversification in the business sector.

During the 1980s, his old friend Jordache, Inc. did end up over-licensing and over-exposing its hot brand. Barriers to entry into the jeans business were relatively low, and competition from a number of big-name manufacturers mounted quickly. The brand did remain popular into the 1990s, but that was about it. It settled down to earth, still selling fairly well, but no longer a must-have item. Wilson took large short positions in Jordache at various points up into the mid-1980s, with mixed results.

The great thing about Jordache stock was that it was always very volatile. One thing that it was never going to do was sit still. Price movement in a stock meant money, and which direction—well, that made no difference, as long as the initial trade was correct.

The Oil Business, 1981 [S]
An Entire Industry Goes off the Cliff

"In 1979, kings were made in the oil business." This old refrain is well remembered, even today. The Shah of Iran fled his country in the first days of that year, and an enormous Mideast oil producer was suddenly in the hands of mysterious crazies of all kinds—to say the least. The ouster of the long-serving, western-backed Shah posed a terrible, destabilizing threat to the entire Middle East. The price of crude oil skyrocketed, of course—threatening $40 a barrel on the spot market.

In 1980, Robert Wilson thought about the old refrain quite often, as he told many friends at the time. Domestic supplies of oil had to be discovered and secured. Everybody in America suddenly seemed to know what a western-states over-thrust belt was; half the country suddenly had come to understand the term "oil wireline." Money was getting people excited—even about geology. Schlumberger, Inc., the lead high-tech prospector for oil in the U.S., was in 1980 a company receiving the kind of public worship that Apple Computer received in the early twenty-first century. In Wyoming, oil-well roughnecks wore T-shirts reading, "If you ain't in oil, you ain't shit."

Robert Wilson had seen many investment frenzies before, usually in individual companies, but this one was on a very grand scale. This was true, industry-wide mania. It was one simple idea, the endless progress of the price of oil, perfect for extremists, and simple-minded extremist thinking. Wilson's targets for short-selling the oil stocks were traditional, conventional, and obvious: the low-margin, no-barriers-to-entry businesses like Nucorp Energy (which just made steel pipe for the industry—mainly in Texas), whose profits would vanish overnight if the price of oil so much as coughed. The only big question was timing. Public speculation in oil stocks was frenzied in 1980; the rubber band was stretching to the breaking point; how much further could things go before the giant bubble burst?

Wilson gave one of his all-time great interviews to Barron's (weekly financial newspaper), at its Year-End Roundtable, at year-end 1980. Calling his investment positions "fabulous," he was short oil stocks across the board. The crummy businesses first, the most vulnerable, the poor operators, the ill-capitalized, the barely profitable even in boom times, but there were many, many names. Wilson was short the very popular Tom Brown Oil, and the man himself soon told the press that "Robert Wilson must not like money."

A year and a half after Wilson's interview with Barron's, in the summer of 1982, all of the oil companies and oil stocks in the country were on the run. In July, 1982, Nucorp Energy filed for bankruptcy protection from creditors. Tom Brown Oil, at least as far as stock price was concerned, looked like the Redwood tree that had returned to the original acorn. The price of a barrel of crude oil had traded above $30 in the frenzied years of 1979-80; by 1986 it was down to near $10. So many oil companies went bankrupt in the early 1980s that the issue came up, for a lot of people: How can the IRS and other government operators tax a short sale of a vanished business? Nucorp Energy, for instance, had gone bankrupt and wafted away into thin air. Robert Wilson and other short-sellers were always obligated to buy back the shares of stock they had sold short, but in this case and others there were no shares to buy back. The business and the stock had gone off into the ether. The IRS did get involved here, particularly, because the huge domestic oil business suddenly had so many bankrupt public companies. The taxmen had to exercise a lot of industry-specific diligence. When a company went bankrupt, that meant, legally, that all investments were "closed out." Wilson and other short-side sharpshooters in the oil patch were considered at that time to have "covered" their short positions, even if no trades were made (and, why would they be?). Otherwise, short-sellers of bankrupt businesses could walk away with 100% of the money they had sold short at the top of the market—with no tax obligations whatsoever. It might be a bit like saying, "Come and get me, copper."

Cable TV and Cablevision, Inc. [L]
Another Big Consumer Revolution

Late in the 1960s, just before Robert Wilson went out on his own as an investor (because of his penchant for large amounts of investment leverage), his good friend Richard Gilder walked into his office at A.G. Becker & Co., New York. Gilder told Wilson, essentially, that the brand-new technology known as cable television was alive, and looked like it was going to take over the world. A very great New York business visionary, Charles Dolan, had won a license in 1965 to wire lower Manhattan for cable TV. Broadcasting conventionally, through the air, to this small and rich area, was impossible, because of the endless tall buildings, which created "the canyons of New York." Dolan called his company Sterling Manhattan Cable. He did not do very well financially, because of the very high cost of laying cable underground, but his efforts caught the eye, and financial support, of corporate titan Time Life, Inc. Dolan started Home Box Office, Inc., no less, at about the same time, and still couldn't make the big money he needed to expand widely as a cable-TV operator. So, he sold both businesses to Time Life.

With the money he had in hand, Dolan dove right back into the cable-TV game. This time he stayed away from Manhattan, and in 1973 started Cablevision, Inc. on suburban Long Island, New York, with 1,500 subscribers. The idea was that middle- and higher-income people would pay for premium television programming, as subscribers on paid networks. The idea was a huge hit, and before long Cablevision expanded into the entire New York metro area; and then into Westchester county to the north, and New Jersey, and Connecticut.

For more than twenty years after its founding, well into the 1990s, Cablevision grew like an unchecked weed. The company expanded into the major markets of Cleveland, Chicago, and Boston, and by the late 1990s had 3.5 million paid subscribers. It became the fifth-largest cable system in the United States. Ultimately, in 2015, the company was sold to the European telecom conglomerate Altice, for just under $18 billion.

Cablevision had gone public in January, 1986, and it is actually not known if Robert Wilson bought in here. 1986 turned out to be his last year as an active investor. The two big public-stock investments in cable television that Wilson owned, from the early 1970s, were Time, Inc., which had bought out entrepreneur Charles Dolan, and Warner Communications, Inc., founded by Steven Ross in 1972. The former investment was indirect, of course, and the second, very direct. Warner Communications had been buying up small cable-TV operators left and right. Chairman Steven Ross (like Charles Dolan) was convinced that narrow-casting to targeted markets, on a paid basis, and not broadcasting generally, would work in television. It was very much the business model suggested and provided by radio. Warner Communications went up against "the big three" television broadcasters of the time, NBC, CBS, and ABC, and did just famously.

Sambo's Restaurants, Inc. [L]
The Turnaround That Wasn't

Sambo's Restaurants, founded in 1957 by two partners, Sam Battistone and Newell Bohnett, was a truly innovative, family-style restaurant company. It expanded wildly across the U.S. in the ensuing twenty years, in large part by offering its individual store managers 20% of a store's profits—a plan known as "Fraction of the Action." Sambo's also developed an employee profit-sharing plan, uniquely generous at the time.

In the 1970s, it seemed that everyone wanted to manage a Sambo's restaurant. None of the other big, national restaurant chains, like McDonald's and Burger King, offered anything like "Fraction of the Action," which was an incredible deal for managers. This generous program fired up the entrepreneurial juices of managers, and caused them to become very dedicated to the business. Sambo's started opening hundreds of new restaurants per year, and by 1979 had over 1,100 hundred of them across the country. Inevitably, management strains were severe; overall growth was just too rapid for the corporate office. Financial pressures became severe as well, because of this over-fast expansion.

On top of everything, political correctness reared its ugly head in the business world, for one of the first times ever. The name "Sambo's" came to be regarded as an anti-black slur, and associated with lawn jockeys, etc. Political pressure forced the company to change the name of many of its stores, especially in the northeastern U.S.

In the fall of 1981, Sambo's filed for bankruptcy. Robert Wilson saw a great pair of innovators, the founders of the company, still presiding and still in charge, and he also thought he saw a Phoenix. Certainly, it was possible that Sambo's could rise from the ashes, with its original management in place. They could light the fire all over again. If Sambo's could get back to first principles, and get its finances in order, the recovery could be a big surprise, and the stock could explode. Wilson moved in, buying one million common shares near $2. This was all a bit like the resurrection of Geico Insurance Company in the late 1970s, in which investor Warren Buffett had seen the possibility of a Phoenix, via a return to first principles, in the auto-insurance business. Buffett purchased seven million shares of Geico, at about $2. He said at the time that he would have purchased more, but he was blocked by insurance regulators.

Geico exploded upward in price, and Sambo's did not. Like Warren Buffett, Robert Wilson had bet on very talented, innovative top management. The cookie didn't crumble his way. As is the case with any investor, many of Wilson's bets did not pan out. The trick is to try always to take no more than small losses, and move on to new opportunities. And there are always new opportunities.

Chrysler Corporation, 1982 [S]
Turning on a Dime

Chairman Lee Iacocca's turnaround, early in the 1980s, of the near-bankrupt Chrysler Corporation—once a proud member of the "Big Three" U.S. auto makers—was a very great achievement. Some business historians consider it to be unique in the history of the auto industry. At the time, next to nobody thought it was possible, including many big, "smart money" investors, like Robert Wilson. Wilson said at the time that short-selling Chrysler stock (at around $5 per share) was like "shooting fish in a barrel."

Chrysler had sought and received a $1 billion loan guarantee from the U.S. government in 1979, not first to stave off bankruptcy, but to save tens of thousands of auto-worker (and related) jobs. It was a politically charged idea and decision, but the U.S. Congress went ahead with it.

Lee Iacocca and his key lieutenants proceeded to center Chrysler's manufacturing efforts on the "K-car platform," which was their own conception, and which underpinned many different models of compact and mid-sized cars, and wagons and minivans. The "platform" allowed huge manufacturing savings, and Chrysler's focus on low- and medium-priced vehicles in the recessionary years of 1981-2 in America turned out to be a winning strategy. The K-car line was profitable for Chrysler Corp. from the very beginning.

Expectations for a trip to zero dollars per share were very heavy, for Chrysler Corp. When the notion first developed in 1982 that things might go the other way, and that the company might actually climb out of its very deep financial hole, it was a moment of truth for many investors, big and small. Peter Lynch of the famous Fidelity Fund, out of Boston, dove on Chrysler's common stock at around $6. Robert Wilson, always tough but always flexible, evidently felt the winds changing direction, and covered fast, eliminating his short position. Perhaps the hard memory of his Resorts International short-sale four years earlier was in play here (see chapter 7), but it is impossible to say. All the evidence indicates that Wilson never traded emotionally, or abandoned first principles.

Under the brilliant strategic planning of Lee Iacocca, Chrysler Corp. just took off, financially and operationally. The company achieved nothing less than a full resurrection. Chrysler paid off its $1 billion in government-guaranteed bank loans early, in just three years, and the common stock eventually rose above $30 per share.

Protecting capital is just as important as making capital. A dollar saved is a dollar earned, etc. There is a great old saying in the investment business: It is always good to know when you are wrong. Another old saying comes to mind: In investing, the bull side doesn't count, and the bear side doesn't count. Only the right side counts.

Apple Computer, 1981 [S]
Never Trust Anyone Over Thirty

Robert Wilson's short position in Apple Computer Corp., off and on during the 1980s, is a bit of a surprise. His short position was a success after 1984, and the temporary hibernation of the great stock bull market of that decade, and the specific information here (which is frankly quite spotty) is that he did fairly well. Wilson knew he was selling short Apple Computer in a bull market, but he was very, very impressed with the dominance of Microsoft Corp. in the personal-computer software market, and the prodigious manufacturing and financial power of the huge IBM Corporation, which made the market-leading personal computer. It was an "IBM-p.c." world, and it was a Microsoft world. Wilson was always generally wary of assuming competitive trouble for any business. But he called Apple Computer "an outsider in an IBM world."

Apple's operating-system business, and all of its related, compatible software applications, running its Macintosh and other personal computers, had about 10% of the personal-computer software market. Microsoft Corp. had the rest, of course, running IBM machines and everything else in "p.c." land. It seems that Robert Wilson differentiated between Apple Computer and, say, Burroughs Computer Corp., or Wendy's Hamburgers, and other former long positions, because Wendy's and Burroughs were not competing in a monopoly-controlled market, whereas Apple really was. Apple Computer Corp. couldn't go anywhere, as no monopoly-dominated business can.

(Much later on, in the 1990s, with the return of Steve Jobs as chairman, Wilson loaded up on Apple Computer stock. The reason was that the company was becoming something completely other, something else. It was not waging war in p.c. software anymore; it was developing entirely new products, including cell phones and then smartphones, that would eventually let it come close to dominating the modern technological world. The common shares Wilson owned did famously.)

Wendy's Hamburgers [L]
Don't Over-Analyze Competition

In fast food, an apparently jam-packed, wildly competitive American market-place, at least since the late 1960s, Wendy's Company, founded in 1969 by Dave Thomas, succeeded prodigiously. Apparently Robert Wilson's first, surprised response here was, "How many hamburgers can America stuff in its face?" Wendy's provided (and reinforced) an important lesson in competitive advantage and disadvantage. Don't assume that rivals showing up will harm a business—just see how competition develops. Wendy's Co. grew fast, and still did no perceptible harm to industry leaders McDonald's and Burger King, etc. These latter two companies were not short sales, nor was Wendy's, as some might (and did) conclude, early on.

In the early 1960s, Robert Wilson had decided shrewdly to buy into Denny's Restaurants, Inc., and ride the giant fast-food blast wave that had originated with McDonald's Corp. (in the mid-1950s). He realized that the same investment policy remained correct, even years later. Do not make guesses about competitive developments, he told himself. Just watch what actually does happen. Wilson stated many times that the single biggest mistake he made as an investor, the mistake that cost him the most money in his career, was worrying about business competition too early. Don't sell out of perfectly good long positions for no good reason. The arrival of competitors often can mean something good: like, an expanding marketplace.

Home Health Care, 1982-3 [L]
Everybody's Getting Old

Early in 1982 Robert Wilson took one of his classic plunges into Superior Care, Inc. and several other in-home health-care stocks. This move was characteristic "new wave" thinking on Wilson's part. The vast baby-boomer generation in America was already starting to roll over and retire, and starting to burden government and private services of all kinds; all the post-war babies were starting to get old, and the demographic numbers going out into the future were indisputable, and truly ominous. This grand U.S. aging trend was only going to intensify. Wilson was a big fan of the in-home health-care business long before the warning sirens really went off, in the 1990s, with such landmark works as Peter G. Peterson's "Gray Dawn," from 1999.

From hindsight far beyond 1982, we know now that the cost of health care is a continuing nightmare; something like a horror movie that will not end. If you want to avoid the worst of health-care expenses, stay away from hospitals. Try to bring health-care services inside the home. These public troubles represented for investor Robert Wilson long-term investment opportunities arguably as good as Datapoint, from the 1960s—but maybe with smaller profit margins. Superior Care, Inc. was just one of the many stocks he bought in this business sector.

Engelhard Minerals [L]
Hiding in Plain Sight

Robert Wilson was not all just mysterious genius and mythical stock-picker. He worked very hard, very steadily, to make money, and that meant that he studied hard, and read and researched constantly. In the end, this meant in turn that he had more and better information than most other investors, even though all the information was public. His efforts allowed Wilson to understand that the giant New Jersey-based company Engelhard Minerals was not really a minerals and ore company, as most everyone assumed, but a trading company. Trading is where the big revenues and profits came from, and not from the other two divisions of the company, ore and precious metals (refining and fabricating). The Philipp Brothers division, derived from an early acquisition by Engelhard, became so big and profitable that by 1981 it accounted for approximately 90% of the company's overall revenues and profits. It was spun off that year, as the famous Phibro Corporation.

The fact that all of this was not well understood, when the Philipp Brothers division was an internal operation, caused Engelhard to be undervalued in the public marketplace, by a large measure. Spot-trading of precious metals and ores, and other scarce resources, had developed into a gigantic global business, starting in the mid-1960s. Philipp Brothers had the biggest and most nimble world-wide trading operation anywhere, and they took and held the lead.

Shearson/American Express, Inc. [L]

Since 1979, Robert Wilson had been telling everybody that he was "furiously bullish" on the U.S. stock market. He used that phrasing, and others that were similarly emphatic. He had a large following in the professional business press, for obvious good reasons, and he kept putting this word out to Barron's weekly newspaper, and Forbes magazine, and The Wall Street Journal, and Business Week magazine, in particular. Wilson put his money where his mouth was by buying into the second-largest brokerage firm in the U.S., Shearson Loeb Rhoades, in 1981. American Express, Inc. purchased the business from founder and chairman Sanford Weill, in April of that year, and Wilson stayed with the new stock, called Shearson/American Express. He liked the new situation very much. The big investment banker and retail-brokerage house remained second only to giant Merrill, Lynch & Co., and now, of course, it had American Express and its deep pockets behind it. Shearson/American Express had more than a quarter of a billion dollars in capitalization, and more than half a billion dollars in annual revenue. Like Wendy's Hamburgers, and Burroughs Computer, and Avis Rent-a Car, for God's sake, these companies were all number-two, and so they had to try harder. Because it was not the market leader, there was also less attention paid to Shearson/American Express, and less respect given it from the investment market. So—more money to be made by investors. Particularly, in the huge new bull market in U.S. stocks that Robert Wilson envisioned.

Buying Shearson/American Express in 1981 represented market timing that was, let us say, impeccable. In the slow, dull, dog days of August, 1982, the U.S. stock market suddenly woke up one morning, and went berserk to the upside. Too many good things had happened, and were happening, in America, to ignore—starting with broadly falling interest rates. These things just could be ignored no longer. The U.S. equity market overnight turned into something like a huge Roman feast, and Shearson/American Express was, of course, right at the center of all the action.

The Dow Jones Industrial Average was around 800 in value, in August, 1982, and—who knew— it was on its way to 18,000.

Memory Metals [S]

Memory Metals, Inc., in the mid-1980s, was one of the sexiest stocks, and businesses, ever seen. It was a small Connecticut-based company with very big plans. Temperature changes could cause certain alloyed metals to change form, and then return to form when temperature also returned to its original level. An electrical heating-and-cooling process was employed, basically, and it looked like these special metal alloys could revolutionize the entire actuator business. Traditional actuators are small solid-state motors, and they are everywhere, physically controlling, in various ways, systems in automobiles, jet engines, spacecraft, biomedical devices, and even robotics. These new-wave "memory metals" were not only lighter and more reliable than conventional actuators, they were also more powerful: enormous energy could be released as they moved back and forth, with changing temperatures.

(Memory metals had been discovered as far back as the 1930s, but only in the 1960s, in a bit of serendipity, did scientists discover and then come to realize that the most effective alloyed metals had real commercial promise. "Memory metals" is actually vernacular for shape-metal alloys. The most effective of these alloys are copper-aluminum-nickel, and nickel-titanium.)

Early in 1986, Memory Metals, Inc. declared, in a series of press releases, that full commercialization of metal-alloy actuators was finally at hand. The company forecast huge growth within one year, to $1.3 million of profits on $16 million in sales. The public, and even professionals, and professional scientists, dove into this unique opportunity, this single public company that was out there, and the thin amount of floating common stock available to everybody. In a matter of weeks, the stock, traded over-the-counter, went from $4 per share to just under $17. Robert Wilson took notice of this situation immediately. He loved the general idea of the business, but he also suspected that the company itself was a phony, or was at least making inflated statements and forecasts. Memory Metals had stated in its recent, glowing press releases that it had huge contracts with major manufacturers, such as Westinghouse, Inc. and Martin Marietta Corp. These declarations were easy to investigate, and they were found to be wanting, to say the least. It looked like the public had become infatuated once again with a wild business idea, in the wild and woolly over-the-counter stock market.

If Wilson hadn't been notified about the 300% move up in Memory Metals' stock by the innumerable stockbrokers hoping to win commission business from him, he would have noticed it himself. Memory Metals was a very exotic product and story, apparently a highly innovative company, and it was making plenty of news. But: too much news.

(Since the 1960s, Wilson had paid out money to brokers, and other stock tipsters, and in great numbers. It was often a full 1% of the stock trades he ended up making. He depended a great deal on incoming advice, although it was less available as time moved on, and the Wall Street investment business changed.

"I'm a derivative thinker. I've never had an original thought in my life," Wilson liked to say.)

In September, 1986, Memory Metals put out what it called a "curative" press release, stating that it had, well, lied to everybody about its business, its sales orders, and its prospects. The stock busted. It went from a high of about $17 down to $6. The shorts, including Robert Wilson, made a ton of money. On the share-price numbers, the situation called to mind TV-tube manufacturer National Video from the 1960s—$4 per share to $55 or so, and then right back down to $4. In the end, in either case, it looked like nothing had happened, but most people who touched Memory Metals stock got clobbered financially, on the way up and also on the way down. A class-action lawsuit was filed against Memory Metals executives, of course. This was the usual short story for Robert Wilson. Just another day at the office.

Shape-metal alloys did represent a genuine technological and scientific break-through, and they had voluminous industrial applications, and implications. The move away from solid-state actuators has actually opened up whole new fields for the actuator. The shape-metal alloys have revolutionized dentistry, particularly orthodontics, and are an important component in the modern smartphone. They are the kind of innovation that Robert Wilson, as an investor, was always looking for. But on the other hand, Memory Metals, Inc. was, quite ironically, a hyped stock—and a sucker's bet. As money-manager Charles Allmon might say, "I like everything about it, except the price."

Cray Research, Inc. [L]
The Cold War Super-Computer

Robert Wilson seemed to know and understand in his bones what Gordon E. Moore, legendary founder of microprocessor-king Intel Corp., and Fairchild Semiconductor, once said, that the number of transistors on a dense integrated circuit—a computer chip—will double every two years, ad infinitum, while simultaneously, the price of same will fall. In other words, the computer was always going to get smaller, and more powerful, and cheaper at the same time, and over time. So, always stay with the computer business, as an investor, because innovation will always be occurring. It is in the very nature of the business.

A new corporate name appeared on the horizon in 1972: Cray Research, Inc., run by the remarkable genius Seymour Cray. Operating out of Wisconsin, and Minneapolis, Cray and his team soon built the fastest supercomputer (mainframe) ever seen. It had a price tag of close to $9 million, and Cray sold it anyway. Cray's new computer was so fast and powerful that it could even forecast the weather, but its real value, and its real appeal, was military. It was for national defense. The Cray computer was so fast that it could conduct data analysis, and run war-games scenarios, like no other mainframe machine. The Cold War was in high gear at the time, and nations of all kinds wanted to perform the fastest and best analysis they could of their enemies lists, and the relevant capabilities.

In a political climate like the Cold War, if you could out-analyze your sovereign enemies on military matters, you gained a lot of real, and also perceived, advantages. Every first- and second-world country suddenly seemed to want a Cray Computer. It was a matter of keeping up, staying abreast, in situations that were possibly life-and-death.

Seymour Cray tried to follow the computer as it made its march toward the inevitable pocket smartphone of 2005, and he introduced the Cray super-minicomputer, but now he encountered competition much more severe than he had for his original, big mainframes.

Robert Wilson and his investment in Cray were long gone, when the Berlin Wall came down in 1989. The end of the Cold War sounded the end for the company, but technology had moved on, and into other hands, well before then. Cray finally closed up shop in 1995. In 1996, it merged its assets with Silicon Graphics, Inc.

Selling Short Resorts International: Big Trouble and a Great Recovery, 1978-80

The Lone Tree That Almost Destroyed the Forest

"This business doesn't get to me—not fundamentally."
WILSON

*"Robert Wilson believes in taking long vacations. But that last vacation
almost wiped out one of America's great stock-market plungers."*
FORBES MAGAZINE, 1979

"On vacation, the only calls I will answer are margin calls."
WILSON

The single investment for which Robert Wilson is most famous did not, in
fact, represent the most interesting or important moment in his career. But
his short sale of 220,000 common shares of hotel operator and New Jersey

casino-gambling company Resorts International, beginning late in 1976 and completed in the spring of 1978, is worth study because it is a harrowing look at the destructive potential of what is commonly known as the statistical outlier.

Wilson had almost a sixth sense for self-protection and self-preservation in the market, as an investor. He took very large positions in many places, obviously in the attempt to make large amounts of money in each position, but it was always in the context of heavy portfolio diversification, heavy short-versus-long hedging, and borrowing money (from his domestic brokers, and from his overseas banks) in carefully calculated amounts.

Resorts International was a short sale that lost money, but it was and is completely unexpected, even to this day, that it lost the money it did (and, relative to Wilson's portfolio value in early 1978). At the time, approaching the end of the 1970s, Wilson had a stock portfolio worth approximately $40 million. His short sale of Resorts International gave him a credit balance of roughly $3.5 million (the stock was sold at an average price of about $16 per share), and the obligation to repurchase 220,000 common shares at some point, any point, in the future.

$3.5 million is a big piece of $40 million. It is almost a full 9%. Nevertheless, Wilson, wildly successful on the short side for well over a decade, clearly thought he could handle it. If any criticism of Wilson's risk management, from hindsight, at this moment could be made, it might be that $40 million is not enough equity to operate with, trading about 250 stock positions hedged short and long, with a total market value of, as a good guess, $200 million. Wilson wanted five-to-one overall leverage (debt) in his portfolio—80% leverage, 20% equity—as he stated many times. He had it. This might be the point of criticism of his overall operation. It would not focus on a 9% equity exposure to obscure, little old Resorts International, Inc. This was a cobra well hidden. Well hidden in tall grass.

Robert Wilson confessed in 1978 that he was tired. He needed rest. He had worked very hard, and for many years, to make money. In fact he considered himself "a money-making machine." He observed that no machine can run flat out forever. There had to be periods of rest. Also, as Wilson pointed out, time away from the stock market would give him time for serious reflection; for the discarding of old views of market trends, and perhaps, for a nascent perception of new trends.

Wilson left the country in April, 1978, on a six-month world tour. His travel itinerary ran to 27 pages. When he arrived at JFK airport in New York, for departure, the ticket agent looked at his enormous ticket envelope and asked him, "Where is your group?" Wilson answered that he was traveling alone. If he looked carefully at his stock portfolio, Wilson could locate Resorts International, among the 200-odd other positions he held. The grand opening of its big new hotel-casino in Atlantic City, NJ was scheduled for May 26. Resorts's common stock was creeping forward, unobtrusively, now to around $20. Wilson was down $900,000 on the position—about 2% of his net worth. He gave an interview to Esquire magazine at this time, and when asked about Resorts he quipped that he "was getting crucified, but might short more." Then he left for the airport. Europe and Scandinavia, India and the Far East, and Australia, beckoned.

Wilson sold Resorts International short at an average $16 per share because he thought it was overvalued at that price, and would come down. Perhaps way down. He had various reasons. There was real doubt, as Wilson began to build his short position, that New Jersey would even allow gambling in the state (a referendum eventually passed, narrowly). Compared with the other casino-gambling companies in the country, all based in Las Vegas, Nevada, of course, Resorts was a richly priced stock. Also, Resorts's big new flagship operation was in a part of the country where the weather wasn't so great—at least not in comparison to Las Vegas. Wilson figured that this would keep a lot of potential customers away. Actual foot traffic would be a lot lower than forecast foot traffic. Additionally, Resorts as a corporation, with its collection of hotels across the country, was not doing well overall in 1978, earning "one phony million dollars a year," as Wilson put it.

There was, unfortunately, another way to look at Resorts International at this point in time. Its major new hotel-casino sat by itself in Atlantic City, NJ, way down the Atlantic coast of the state, uncontested as a casino-gambling operation. At least for the time being. The hotel's "competitors" were not that—they were more than 2,000 miles away in the western desert. Resorts in New Jersey could almost be considered a monopoly. Perhaps it was or would become a de facto monopoly. A monopoly position would mean it could charge plenty for all kinds of things—parking, hotel rooms, meals—that its Nevada cousins could not. And this hotel-casino had an enormous potential market surrounding it—the heavily populated Northeast and East of the U.S. A very large region full of people who had never gambled legally before, and might be hungry to try out something exciting and completely new. Additionally, the weather in New York and New Jersey, etc. was not that bad—there were a couple of tough months in the winter, but nothing worse than that. A final point: the state of New Jersey, and its Casino Gaming Commission, were determined to help Resorts International make things work: they were determined to try to revive economically moribund Atlantic City. It was a famous old resort town down south on the ocean, that in fact had many different kinds of businesses on location, in need of help. A big hotel and casino at the center of town could provide a huge economic shot in the arm to Atlantic City, and to the surrounding region. Government was behind this business effort.

In June, 1978, a month after opening its Atlantic City casino, Resorts International reported initial results. Lines were around the block and out of sight, to get inside the main building and to get at the big casino. It was not a formal earnings report that the company delivered, but clearly Resorts International's new business was strong—shockingly strong. Like no advance report in its previous, ten-year history. The public poured into the common stock, just as they had started pouring onto Resorts International's large hotel-casino grounds in famous old "A.C.," New Jersey.

It appeared very quickly that Robert Wilson was in trouble. Certainly he was losing large sums of money, every day the American Stock Exchange (in New York) was open, and Resorts's common stock was trading. He had sold short his entire position of 220,000 shares over many months, between $9 and $20, and now the whole thing was moving against him. Wilson was among the most unemotional and dispassionate of men, as his friends and associates always observed, and his first thoughts about a rising Resorts International stock price went to his original reasons for selling the stock short—his due diligence, conducted before taking the short position in the first place. Not to the rising stock price. Wilson didn't see any reason to change his original views or investment position. The excitable American public was just getting excited about a stock. It had happened thousands of times before.

Wilson kept moving across northern Europe, to the capital city Oslo and then into the gorgeous Norwegian fjord country. And the price of Resorts kept rising. Before leaving on vacation, he had sold short his last batch of Resorts stock, at around $20 per share. That was in March. In June, it traded at $80. Wilson had lost more than $10 million, in a single stock, and he was only worth about four times that much. He was in a lot of out-of-the-way places in northern Europe, and hard to reach, but Neuberger and Berman, his brokers in New York, who handled his short sales of stock almost exclusively, did reach him eventually, and persuaded him to start covering, buying in, some Resorts shares—at $81.

Wilson kept traveling, out of Europe and into South Asia, and then across India. And things back home started to get a lot worse. In July, Resorts's stock crossed above $100 per share. Wilson determined to stick it out. This was just a popular madness based on little, or nothing. The stock market in the U.S. had been so bad for so long, and "investors" had lost so much money in so many different false hopes and dreams over the years, that they were diving on the gambling stocks, believing that El Dorado had finally come into view. Wilson called Neuberger and Berman in New York, and told them to call his bankers in Switzerland, and to effect wire transfers for whatever money they needed to meet margin calls in his stock account with them. Resorts International, once 3% of Wilson's overall short position, had reached a full third of that position. 33%! It was metastasizing, growing leaps and bounds, a cancer growing on and all over his portfolio.

Still the idea of El Dorado would not go away. In late July, Neuberger and Berman, as brokers, started to worry about Wilson's huge losses as a threat to their own capital. They gave their star client a loss-limit beyond which he could not go. Wilson agreed. Throughout July and into August, Resorts stock just went nuts. It went from $120 to $180 per share in a single week! This was nonsense, just another tulip-o-mania, right out of seventeenth-century Holland. Wilson got to Taiwan in early September, and the usual grim cables from New York were waiting for him at his hotel. He called New York back, and called it quits. To hell with it. He closed out the Resorts International position completely. His final purchase was for 45,000 shares at $187—more than $8 million. It was over.

It might be hard to understand why, but Robert Wilson's reaction to his capitulation and loss here was unlike anyone else's. His friends back home who were in the know, and his brokers back home, were just devastated. The semi-informed press back home started chortling. In total, in Resorts, he had dropped $24 million. $20 million of it in 1978 alone. Wilson quipped, "I've slipped on a banana peel. I've done it before, and I'll do it again. It's the nature of the business."

What the hell could that possibly mean? What it meant, actually, was that Wilson's very big investment game was all about percentages, and averages. And Wilson was, in fact, O.K. He had lost a terrifying $24 million in Resorts International, more than 80% of it in this one stock in a matter of a few months, and he was only worth $42 million at the start of 1978. The loss that year was almost 50% of his entire capital. 50%! But Wilson, always hedged and always diversified, had made a crucial $6 million at the same time, on his many other investments—principally on the long side. Wilson's net loss for 1978 was $14 million, not $20 million. He did not have just $22 million left, he had $28 million left. The loss was very newsworthy, but it wasn't all that bad.

"Just a third," Wilson quipped.

Wilson had taken his long vacation to Europe and Asia to rest himself, and also to think hard about Wall Street and its major trends, what he might be thinking wrong about the business, and what new major trends might be emerging. Only with great distance could perspective come. July, 1978, the worst single month ever for Wilson's stock portfolio, ironically turned out to be, in Wilson's estimation, one of the best months ever for the United States. Over the objections of the left-wing (or left-leaning) President Jimmy Carter, the U.S. Congress significantly cut the capital-gains tax rate! Wilson could not believe the news at first. He had to conclude nothing less than that the U.S., after so many bad economic years, really an entire decade, was going to throw off its socialist trends and directions and policies, and get back to capitalism. The U.S. was sick of its "emerging second-world status," as Wilson put it. The country felt insecure, and that made it angry. The country was going to stop redistributing wealth, from producers to non-producers, and takers, and start rewarding investment, and private business development, and production.

In the summer of 1978, Wilson turned almost at once from a famous bear into a raving bull. It was "U-Turn Wilson" all over again. With the cut in the federal capital-gains tax, he believed that the United States economy was going to start moving forward again. And he would position his stock portfolio accordingly. He finished his travels and arrived back in Los Angeles in October, and he said then that he felt like he had never left. He also said at the time that his psyche felt completely different, nevertheless. He could see the U.S. economy not as moribund, but as already having turned some giant corner to the upside.

Over the course of the next two years, Wilson's "psyche" proved to be correct, as it had so many times in the past. As a simple matter of history, almost all stock bull markets begin imperceptibly, or at least unobtrusively, coming out of a serious low point, and then quietly advancing forward. Prices will only start accelerating from higher levels. The public will generally not get involved in a new bull market until more than half of the gains are already made. Wilson could sense a gathering bull market way, way early. In 1979, he made a net $21 million. It was a fantastic, 70% gain. A grand recovery from the Resorts trouble.

He went that year from a net worth of $28 million, to $49 million. In 1980, he was up another 60%, to $81 million. The last thing Wilson was was gun-shy, from his trouble in 1978. Becoming gun-shy would have been an abandonment of investing and operating principles, and a huge error. $81 million at the end of 1980 was basically three times what Wilson had two years earlier. It was gigantic money, and it represented tremendous power to do more. Resorts International from 1978 had turned into an amusing little flickering fire, distant in his rear-view mirror.

Going Large: $100 Million in Net Worth, and Beyond

*"My goal is to make a billion dollars. I may not
get there; the important thing is to try."*
WILSON

Late in 1981, the U.S. stock market got hit hard to the downside. Robert Wilson had been doing O.K., but nothing like his big year in 1980, or the even bigger year of 1979. He ended up with a paltry gain of $4 million. Five percent. His net worth climbed from $81 to $85 million in 1981. But he continued to sense that big things were afoot, for the economy, for the country, and for the stock market. Big, positive things. It seemed no coincidence to Wilson that the pro-business and anti-government President Ronald Reagan had been swept into office in a landslide vote a year earlier. Wilson continued to maintain an overall stock position of 80% net long—the exposure to the market of his net worth, and his gross exposure to the market as well (figuring in leverage and borrowing). For every $100 worth of stocks he had sold short, he owned $500 of other stocks. He held them long. Wilson had been in this aggressively bullish posture since late 1978. A few months after positioning this way he had told the press that he was "so bullish, whatever speed bumps come along, they are not going to make any difference at all."

Many of the stocks that Wilson owned at this time were technology stocks. He saw the United States as starved for economic growth; and he saw the solution to that problem to be productivity increases. To Wilson, productivity meant one thing before anything else: high-technology companies. They were the lead providers of productivity; it was in the nature of their businesses. These companies could improve performance and lower costs, at the same time, like nobody else. Wilson told Barron's that "[technology businesses] are the engines of our progress now."

1981 had been a very important financial year, noted by many on Wall Street, because very high American interest rates had finally peaked, and started to head down. Paul Volcker, chairman of the Federal Reserve Board, had put so much monetary pressure on the ruinous situation that the rate fever had in fact been broken. Rates on the 30-year U.S. Treasury bond had come within a whisker of 16%. But that was it. That was in fact the end, the top. Bond prices could start to come off of the floor, and it might even become possible with lower interest rates to justify higher price-earnings multiples for stock prices. Maybe.

1982 arrived. The U.S. stock market crept forward, rising slowly out of its nasty low from the fourth quarter of 1981. Spring was quite uneventful. President Reagan and his team were working hard on economic and financial matters, and had pushed through new laws lowering domestic taxes. The Dow Jones Industrial Average was drifting sideways, just under the 800 level. August arrived. The middle of the month approached. It was dullsville in the American investment world. The dog days of summer had arrived. Many people were away on vacation, and stock trading, on the big exchanges and over-the-counter, was very light.

On August 17, for no particular reason, the U.S. stock market erupted like a battleship at dawn. The explosion in the volume of shares traded was as dramatic as the mind-boggling increase in share prices. Trading volume more than doubled, instantly, from recent average levels, and the broad market indices started gaining as much as 3% in a single day. The action was unrelenting—day after day, week after week, all the way into October, 1982, before taking a rest. The Dow Jones Industrial Average leapt forward about 40% from its mid-summer low, to a level approaching 1200. The great 1980s bull market was underway. There was no question about it. Robert Wilson got off one of his great one-liners, right here: "The bears have nothing left but their telephones!"

1982 was a very special year for Wilson, in particular, because he achieved one of his cherished long-term goals: $100 million in net worth. Nine figures. The calculations were made at year-end, as usual, and there the number was: $110 million net. Up $25 million for the year, which was a very satisfactory gain of just under 30%. This was an awful long way from getting wiped out in 1956; it was an awful long way from his net worth of $15,000, in 1958. $100 million was just a towering achievement. On a percentage-return basis, it was an achievement that was and is unique; untouched. It was cause for celebration; a big celebration. It was cause for a big party, to be hosted by Robert Wilson himself.

Early in 1983 Wilson was riding very high. He had driven his net worth to nine figures, and he could celebrate at home, no less, in grand style. He had gotten a divorce in 1977 and moved from Brooklyn to Manhattan, and then in 1978 purchased a huge apartment on the sixteenth floor of the San Remo Building, high up on Central Park West. More than 150 feet above the street, his views of the Park were unparalleled. He had purchased this apartment, more than 5,000 square feet in size, for the incredible sum of $300,000. (It would end up rising to seventy or eighty times that value, after 2010.) Once again, he had made a purchase at a low point in the market.

Wilson invited about sixty of his friends and associates to his home, one night early in 1983—black tie required. He served his own specialty Martinis, and the usual large appetizers. He liked telling his guests at his (many) cocktail parties that they could eat heartily when he was in charge, and not have to go out to dinner later. Eminently practical.

In 1979, Wilson had told the press that for the first time in his life, he enjoyed socializing more, and working less. His move to Manhattan two years before he described as nothing less than "glorious." Certainly in 1983, his own big party hit a very high note for him. Emphatically, he was now one of the "rich professional money men," as author John Train put it. And he had done it all under his own steam.

1983 was also a great investment year for Wilson. He remained 80% net long stocks, and many of them were technology stocks—the market's leaders. The bull market momentum from 1982 kept surging. He was up $63 million more in 1983, to a total net worth of $173 million. It was a gain of almost 60%—way ahead of the market averages.

In January, 1984, the U.S. bull market had its first big break to the downside—its first big "correction," in brokerage-industry parlance. The market then went sideways to up for the balance of the year. Wilson dropped $19 million in 1984. He went from a net worth of $173 million down to $154 million. It was, for Wilson, a warning sign, the way any losing year always was. Specifically, he had told himself many years earlier, when in his forties, that if he failed to outperform the broad stock-market averages for three years running, he would quit the investment business. This reflected his marvelous, oft-stated observation that "investors are like athletes." In other words, like any athlete, even the greatest investor can and will one day lose a step, and start to wear out. The metaphor here is about athletes, and machinery. Neither should be run flat-out; there must be periods of rest. And second, no athlete and no machine can last forever.

1985 was a good year for Wilson, a gainer. But it was still another sub-par year. This fact just appalled him. His relative performance truly seemed to be lagging, and flagging. He went from $154 million net worth to $197 million that year, almost a 30% gain, but the stock averages were slightly ahead of him. In 1986 he gained another $33 million, to $230 million at year-end, but in May of that year he sent out a letter to about one hundred stock brokers and friends, telling them that he was in the third year of underperforming the broad stock-market averages. With extreme self-discipline, he announced in the letter that that was it. He was gone; done. He was quitting. Babe Ruth had lost his touch; Jesse Owens had lost a step; Mighty Casey had struck out.

"Sooner or later, everybody fucks up," Robert Wilson always liked to say. It was one of his favorite observations. As a board member of the Whitney Museum of American Art, in New York City, he would apply it to his museum director, Tom Armstrong, who was fired in 1990; now, four years earlier, he applied it to himself.

Wilson made a couple of great statements to the press at this time, among others. "What the hell is the point of working your ass off if you can't beat the market averages?" he asked. "I'll just put all of my money in an index fund!" He also said, "You either work at this business eighteen hours a day, or you don't work at it."

It is a most interesting point here that Wilson quit as a professional investor because of performance issues alone. So many other people hang on in jobs that have out-run them, simply because they have "nothing else to do," and "nowhere else to go." There is no logic in this thinking, only dangerous and emotional self-delusion, and Wilson knew these truths cold, and acted on them immediately. Not having something else to do has nothing to do with getting out of a business you are no longer very good at, or good enough at. Go find something else to do later on. Don't keep under-performing, or worse, digging a hole for yourself. Quit what you're doing. Whatever the particular circumstances, that move will always be correct. Go out into the park and watch the birds, and then think about the future.

Robert Wilson at career-end was a lot like golfer Jack Nicklaus, at the same crossroads. Nicklaus won his last major golf championship, the Masters, in 1986, when he was 46 years old. He kept playing for a number of years afterward, but eventually he told the press, "I will keep playing pro golf as long as I can be competitive. If you're in a golf tournament and you're not competitive, then you're just walking around out there on the grass." It is no surprise that these comments come from an athlete.

Robert Wilson was very bullish on U.S. stocks, and the U.S. in general, in 1986, and he viewed himself that year simply as a tired old bull who would hand off his terrific sum of investment capital to a considerable number of younger, talented bulls, who could run with it, for standard money-management fees. It is no surprise that diversification, and hedging of long positions, were at all times required by Wilson here. It was his money, and he would shape and direct its management. He ended up hiring twenty different hedge-fund money managers whom he felt looked at the stock market the way he did, and whose investment track records he admired. (He would end up firing a few of them from time to time in the future; and these operators shall remain nameless.) Wilson had been bullish on stocks since late in 1978, and he often said that he believed, looking back, that the U.S. equity market had actually turned from bearish to bullish at the super low late in 1974, when the Dow Jones Industrial Average broke below 600. The decisions and requirements and hirings declared by Robert Wilson, once he retired, turned out to be crucial, and correct. In spite of the one-day "crash of 1987," and a very severe stock-market low late in 1990, Wilson's twenty bullish money-managers ran his net worth from just above $200 million in 1986 to the grand total of $800 million, by the year 2000. Wilson rarely set a foot wrong in his career, and he certainly didn't do it this time, either. (Stock-market forecaster James Finucane, who has been mentioned earlier, declared late in 1990 that the U.S. stock market was in the best and most powerful low since 1974; and that the 1990 low might even be equivalent (in quality, and severity) to the 1974 low. This observation proved correct; the stock market went straight up for the next ten years.)

Wilson had always wanted to be a billionaire, and now he was achingly close. But he was also 73 years old. And, one day early in the new millennium, he had a meeting with his old friend Roger Hertog. Hertog was a famous New York City philanthropist, a very active one, who had great affection for and focus on the arts and the humanities, in particular. Robert Wilson's meeting with Roger Hertog would re-direct him completely.

Throwing Things in Reverse: Big-Time Philanthropy

"Bob [Wilson] saw the world for what it is, dreamed of what it could be, and he would let nothing deter his drive to make it so."
FRED KRUPP, PRESIDENT, ENVIRONMENTAL DEFENSE FUND

"We are put on this earth to be productive."
INVESTOR JAMES FLANAGAN

"There is plenty of everything in this country, except one thing: cash."
INVESTOR CHARLES ALLMON

Back at the beginning of 1987, Robert Wilson was at a major crossroads in his life. He was a unique man and a unique worker, and thus not surprisingly, unlike almost everybody else in the same situation, this moment did not bother him. He wasn't sure what road to take next, but he did know that he had stopped running down the wrong road. A very good friend commented to Wilson that he might now be in his "princely phase," and would perhaps start helping others financially, rather than helping himself in the marketplace.

As noted earlier, Wilson had always done "tithing," as he called it. He had always been willing to give some money away, to worthy causes, even at the beginning of his career. Out of the day-to-day investment business, now he also spent considerable time fulfilling responsibilities as a board member of both the New York City Opera, and the Whitney Museum of American Art. He had been on the board at both organizations since the early 1980s; and in 1981 he became chairman of the board, New York City Opera. Wilson also served on the board of the New York Metropolitan Opera. All of these institutions required financial support, of course, and Wilson obliged. That was expected of board members before anything else.

It is a famous story that in 1989 a donation card, from a direct-mail campaign, reached Wilson at his home on Central Park West. It asked for $25, for the World Monuments Fund, based in New York City. Wilson thought about it for a while and then he sent back a check for $5,000. "I like monuments," he used to say. Perhaps right here he was becoming more inclined toward philanthropy than before.

The 1990s arrived. There was a very severe U.S. stock-market low late in 1990. The Clintons arrived in the White House in 1993; and all the while, Robert Wilson and his money-managers remained bullish on America, and American business. This strategic position was correct. The stock market went on what would turn out to be a ten-year run to the upside, out of the 1990 low. Wilson had nearly another net $600 million added to his fortune, making a grand total of $800 million by the year 2000.

As mentioned above, around this time, at the turn of the millennium, Robert Wilson's old friend Roger Hertog, a famous New York philanthropist with a particular focus on the arts and humanities, went out to lunch with him and asked him why he wasn't giving his money away. The suggestion to become a major philanthropist, not just a minor one, gave Wilson pause, and for his own very good reason. "My sense of self-worth is tied up to a significant degree with my net worth," he liked to say, usually with a grin. He also made the unassailable statement, "I know so many people who have given money away, and they've done more harm than good."

But Wilson had demonstrated for decades that he could change his mind in a hurry, even on the most critical issues. In investing, this was nothing less than a matter of survival, and then prosperity. But this great principle seemed to apply to other endeavors, as well; even to considerations of how to live.

But, again, the question was a big one: Why give money away? Wilson loved being rich, and had always hated spending. He stated that the first appeal of philanthropy for him was that it was, truly, investing. Like an investor, a philanthropist would have to do much due diligence, to select the right recipients, the right "donees"; he would have to build gift "positions," and not create them all at once; he would certainly want to take some risks, to get good new things going; and most exciting of all for Robert Wilson, particularly operating out of New York City, he could challenge other people to get involved in making gifts with him. This last had of course been his favorite thing, as a stock-market investor: leverage. Using lots of other people's money, to accomplish what you will.

It is important to recognize that while Wilson did not plan in advance to become a major philanthropist, his more modest giving was quite steady, before and after his retirement in 1986. So his transition from investing to philanthropy was a bit of an extended, and osmotic process. His full acceleration into the effort and occupation of philanthropy took quite a bit of time. It did not hurt the process at all, of course, that hundreds of millions of fresh dollars had been pouring into his various investment accounts.

The place where Wilson made his first really big donation was the New York Public Library: first under the direction of Paul LeClerc, and then Anthony Marx. The grand institution centered on Fifth Avenue and 42nd Street, New York City, and with many outlying branches. Wilson had actually started contributing to the Library early in the 1980s. Wilson said about his gifts to the library, "I want my money to do a little bit of good for a lot of people." He positively treasured information and knowledge, which had always been so important to him in his career, and he was determined to make information more accessible to, and learning easier for, the public at large. This meant collecting information, and preserving it, and distributing it by best means available. A major tactic here was electronic capture, and then digitization, of vast amounts of the Public Library's vast storehouse of knowledge—whatever its original form.

Wilson made a huge contribution to the expansion of the Public Library's website, and its on-line (and on-time) offerings of information; and he also made possible for the first time the examination and inventorying and processing of the library's vast archives. No one had even looked at them in decades. Library president Paul LeClerc said at the time that Wilson's gifts allowed the evaluation (and considerable digital conversion) of 20,000 linear feet of file boxes! End to end, these file boxes could run four miles in length! It was a priceless advance for the library and the public, really, and it was possible only because of countless man-hours of effort, purchased with very large amounts of money.

Wilson "built" his philanthropic position in the New York Public Library over four different decades, eventually contributing a total of $40 million. His money did what he wanted it to do, which was to effect major changes for the good, in a place that was vitally important.

Even in the 1990s Wilson stated that the things that concerned him most, as someone who was able to help out financially, were those things that were perishable, and at risk; that needed money in a timely fashion as a matter of survival itself. These were, most importantly, the natural environment, wildlife, and the "built" world of man-made monuments. The world of man-made monuments was at risk first because of myriad politically motivated evil-doers around the world, monument destroyers, who often seemed to be as plentiful as grand monuments themselves, both ancient and modern. Wilson said more than once, "If I don't contribute right now, if I don't help out right now, [it] won't be there anymore." Time was indeed money, in a special way.

What begins to appear in any study of Robert Wilson's philanthropy is the fact that he did not give money idly to things that interested and entertained him; the center of his giving was always to particular things, and the causes behind them, that would improve the world. Wonderfully, Wilson's giving was never about him, and it was not about pet projects; it was about the things that he believed most needed and deserved support, to make the world a better place for everybody. That is the simple truth.

A very rich and urbane man, evidently he cared a great deal about the poor and disadvantaged. He was for more than forty years a major backer of the American Civil Liberties Union, particularly in its fight against the egregious and unnecessary incarceration of non-violent drug offenders. Wilson hated the Rockefeller drug laws of New York state, which were a huge overreaction to a big drug problem from the 1970s, and that caused untold, unnecessary pain. Politicians as late as President Obama have still tried to unravel and eliminate them (unfortunately, other states followed the New York model).

Wilson certainly believed, as many people do, that one of the best investments a person can make is in young people. These ones are inheriting the earth, and their development and education are very significant matters. Wilson was led to start providing major money to the Catholic schools of New York City, through the New York Archdiocese; there were severe financial problems in the parochial-school system, and a lot of schools were failing and closing down. Wilson thought the Catholic schools were the best part of the vast New York City school system. He stated that these schools shaped character, and pounded home obligation to the less fortunate—and did not just teach the three Rs. For Wilson, this was a crucial attribute that made them distinctive, and distinctly worthy.

In consultation with friend and New York philanthropist Roger Hertog, Robert Wilson made the momentous decision, after the year 2000, to pledge 70% of his net worth to charity. He was not going to try for a net worth of $1 billion, after all. It was a long-held and cherished goal, but now it appeared to be the wrong move. Wilson changed his mind—as he had so often in his career, concerning other investments.

70% was a number common to many very large pledges; a kind of philanthropic norm. In Wilson's case, this meant a pledge of $560 million—70% of his $800 million. In 2002 he set up a trust to handle his disbursements to charities. The great English theologian C.H. Spurgeon once said, "Money is easy to make, and difficult to spend wisely." It is certainly fair to say here that Wilson wholeheartedly agreed with this observation. He would exercise all due diligence, just as in his investing days, and build a diversified, hand-picked portfolio of many different gifts. He would build it over time; it would be important not to give too quickly or too slowly, depending on the particular institution or organization receiving money. There would be, Wilson decided, a core, a base, of three or four seasoned and established charities that were going to endure, and that he could help to expand—in consultation with them—in significant new ways—in significant new areas. Investing in stocks was similar to, but of course not the same as, philanthropy. There was no longer a way Wilson could "sell short" to protect his "long investments"—all his gifts to charity by definition would be a matter of spending, and ownership. Similar to "long" positions in the stock market. So, as insurance, this time, Wilson wanted to put the bulk of his gifted money into well established charities that had been around a long time, and would be around tomorrow, and the day after that.

Wilson settled on a plan to give $100 million each to four big charities. (About $200 million of his pledged $560 million would thus remain for others.)

A key part of his thinking here, beyond the safety of big organizations, was leverage. If he put up nine figures, several different times, he could bring enormous psychic, public pressure to bear on other philanthropists, to "match" his gifts. If he pledged $100 million to a famous, worthy cause, he could probably end up getting a total of $200 million to the charity. (In the case of the World Monuments Fund, out of New York, he was actually able to get more.) He would deliver as much as $100 million, in other words, in the form of matching grants. It was sort of like his old investing days—but the leverage would not be quite as extensive. He could only require a "match," and get 50%. In the old days he worked with 80% leverage, of course, but that was a different game.

Robert Wilson's first concerns, evidently, were conservation and preservation; and that included preservation of the "built" world, the world of man-made monuments. Here is a look at the "big four" organizations that he settled upon:

The Nature Conservancy

This organization, based in Arlington, Virginia, was founded in 1951, and it is the largest of its kind in the U.S. Today it has more than one million members, and operates across America and in seventy countries around the world. The Nature Conservancy prides itself on being directed by science alone; not politics, or anything else. Its large-scale conservation projects are directed at entire ecosystems, and are indicated by scientific analysis of needs. TNC states that it is concerned with everything from "coral reefs to deserts;" and plants and animals, and rivers and lakes and oceans.

There is an intelligent, overt effort to be non-confrontational, and by this TNC means working with indigenous peoples wherever possible, and enlisting their help in conserving their local environment and wildlife.

Environmental Defense Fund

Founded in 1967, and based in New York City, this organization started small, and became very big and influential, principally under the long-term leadership of president Fred Krupp. Like the Nature Conservancy, it was always concerned with science, and the rational policy of letting science direct its best efforts, to protect the environment.

Long before it became a popular cause, the Environmental Defense Fund was concerned with excessive carbon emissions, and "greenhouse gases," and global warming. For instance, EDF has for a long while made major efforts to use financial incentives to curb fire use, in deforestation of the Amazon jungle. It is as concerned with the intense carbon emissions there as the loss of tree mass.

EDF is also making major efforts to battle farm pollution—mainly, fertilizer runoff and its pollution of rivers and ponds and lakes. It is interested in chemical-policy reforms in general, which it is sure will do nothing less than make households safer. Food development is another of EDF's concerns. Using science and technology, always, how is it best to proceed? How do people maximize food yields, in a safe farming operation?

World Monuments Fund

Founded in 1965, this organization is the world leader in its field. To date it has protected, preserved, and restored more than six hundred monuments around the world from the depredations of time, weather, natural disasters, and bad people intent on destruction. WMF is always on the lookout for acute problems and needs—threats to monuments that are time-critical. It has been focused, formally, on acute problems since 1995.

WMF is interested in incorporating training programs into all of its field projects, to enlist effective local support for monuments when WMF arrives, and after it is gone.

The monuments preserved and restored are endlessly varied. WMF has granted its designations to the grandest structures in the world, and also to a structure as small and interesting (and vulnerable) as the Discovery Hut, on Ross Island by McMurdo Sound, Antarctica, used in the first years of the twentieth century by Commander Robert F. Scott, in his two attempts to reach the South Pole.

Late in 2013, Bonnie Burnham, president of WMF, said that "[Robert Wilson] became the match king of the philanthropic world."

Wildlife Conservation Society

The Society, based at the Bronx Zoo in New York, was founded originally as the New York Zoological Society, in 1895. Today it has five hundred field-conservation projects going on around the world, on two million square miles of land, in more than sixty countries. There are two hundred scientists on staff at WCS. The Society, like the Nature Conservancy, has more than one million members.

When Robert Wilson first got involved with WCS, as a benefactor, it was out of a particular concern for Africa, the greatest wildlife continent. WCS had a division running its international operations (Wildlife Conservation International, which became the Global Conservation Program) that was not as strong operationally or financially as WCS was in North America. Wilson actually spent $250,000 of his own money to run a test, for himself, before possibly committing much larger sums to WCS. In the early 1990s he sent three scientists to Africa for two months, to examine WCS's conservation operations in depth. The report came back to Wilson that WCS in Africa could deploy big money well—that it had the infrastructure, and personnel on the ground—but that various changes and improvements were needed. Wilson shared the findings of his scientists and their investigation with WCS, and the organization accepted them, agreed to most of them, and Wilson got on board full time with WCS from that point forward.

The Wildlife Conservation Society, like Robert Wilson's other "big four" charities, runs operations with considerable economy of effort. It has targeted efforts in fifteen key regions of the world; wild-animal habitats containing roughly 50% of all the world's bio-diversity. As a largely political matter, the Society has also chosen to protect big, iconic wildlife species: gorillas, tigers, elephants, whales, etc. The idea here is that protecting "the famous" will help protect all bio-diversity, and ecosystems, as well.

Robert Wilson ultimately directed $400 million of his own money to preservation and conservation around the world; but as he always had, he wanted diversification. There were, of course, large classes of people everywhere who were in need. He had great concern for the young people of New York City, and their education. The city's public-school system was vast: 1.1 million students. The largest in the country. What could Wilson do? Exactly where could he direct a big piece of money, enough money to make a serious difference, and improvement?

In 2007, he came upon the idea of the Catholic schools of New York City, and for the stark reason that they "teach virtue." How to behave, how to treat others, how to be a responsible and constructive member of society. Not just the three Rs. Wilson thought that the Catholic schools at least did a better job than the average public school; the "unionized schools" of New York City, as he called them. (Teachers'-union schools.) Robert Wilson said that he always valued "virtue" in every person. He said more than once that he considered it the only thing more important than money!

Declaring that Catholic schools all over the country were crumbling and closing, and that "Bill Gates probably doesn't have enough money to save them," Wilson's giving to the New York parochial-school system went above $10 million in short order, and then kept going. Eventually, it caught the attention of the Archdiocese, and of Edward Cardinal Egan himself. The Archdiocese contacted Wilson, and requested a meeting. Wilson demurred. Then, a little while later, he agreed. He would meet with the Cardinal. The Cardinal presented Wilson with a book on opera, and that broke the ice. Wilson told him that he was an atheist; the Cardinal replied that he would work to convert him. Wilson could not resist replying that he might convert the Cardinal, but that then, "you'll lose your job." A strong friendship was born.

Before he was done, around 2012, Wilson had given New York City's Catholic schools $45 million.

At night, when the (home) financial markets were closed, Robert Wilson could very often be found at the opera. Arguably the most complex of all art forms, opera had fascinated him for most of his life. Very frequently, he would take trips to Europe, and go on opera-viewing tours, and then make detailed write-ups of each production he had seen. At home in New York, he was on the board of the grand Metropolitan Opera, but in classic Wilson fashion, his strongest focus was actually on number two: the New York City Opera. Founded in 1943, New York mayor Fiorello La Guardia had called it "the people's opera": it would appeal to wide audiences, and offer very reasonable ticket prices.

Wilson had an unshakable instinct for the second tier, as an investor and as a philanthropist. Clearly he believed, as an investor, that more money could be made by ignoring the market's leaders; and as a philanthropist, he clearly sensed that he could get more done on the second tier of public institutions, and that his donated monies would go much further.

Wilson was a board member and steady contributor to the NYC Opera in the 1970s, and particularly after his big move to Manhattan in 1977. In 1981, he was elected chairman of the board. These were the years of General Director Beverly Sills, who served in that capacity from 1979 to 1988. Sills did a great deal to restore NYC Opera's financial health from previous low points, but financial trouble started to return after she left. By 1993, when lawyer and philanthropist Irwin Schneiderman was appointed co-chairman of the board of NYCO, he stated that his job was "simply to save the opera."

Robert Wilson left the NYCO chairmanship in 1993, but he continued to give the opera several million dollars every year. It was badly needed money, and everybody knew it. After 2001, there was a lot of talk at the NYCO about leaving home, the New York State Theater at Lincoln Center, because of money difficulties, and moving downtown—perhaps to a grand new cultural center at the old World Trade Center site.

Robert Wilson established his charitable trust in 2002, vested with $560 million—70% of his net worth. Irwin Schneiderman approached him and asked him if, at the age of 75 now, he might consider a major gift to his great love, the New York City Opera. A gift that would make it possible for the NYCO to move downtown, into a grand new space of its own. Schneiderman asked Wilson for $75 million. (A nice number, to match his age.) Wilson looked at Schneiderman, and said, "No." Then Wilson kept looking at Schneiderman. He let the seconds tick by. Schneiderman became a bit agitated (this is all according to his own account). He thought Wilson was saying no, for real: in other words, zero new money for NYCO. Then, Wilson answered him, with a grin: "But I can do fifty." Fifty million dollars! (Schneiderman is fond of saying that Robert Wilson "liked to torture his donees. Yes, he's very good at that.")

The pledge of $50 million from Wilson was for real, but shortly afterward NYCO's situation became impossible. It continued to hemorrhage money as an operation, and then it was beaten out for space at the World Trade Center site by other arts groups. The severe recession and real-estate collapse of 2008 sounded the death knell for the great old company. A move downtown became just impossible, and in 2011 NYCO moved out of Lincoln Center, and then moved its offices to lower Manhattan. By late 2013, the company was bankrupt.

As much as Robert Wilson loved monuments, he retained great affection for the pictorial arts. He had been on the board of the Whitney Museum of American

Art, in New York, since the late 1970s. In the 1990s he became Vice-chairman, under Chairman Leonard Lauder, the museum's most important benefactor, whose gift of $131 million in 2008 made a huge move to lower Manhattan, and into a new building, possible.

The Whitney was founded in 1930, and in 1966 moved to Madison Avenue and 75th Street, New York City. It was an innovative organization; it was the first museum to establish small, corporate-funded "branch" museums—three in New York, and a fourth in Connecticut. In 2015, thanks to Chairman Lauder, the Whitney moved to a grand new location: a steel and glass and concrete beauty in the meat-packing district of lower Manhattan, hard by the Hudson River. The designer was world-renowned architect Renzo Piano. Vice Chairman Robert Wilson had given such a considerable sum of money to the Whitney Museum over the years that it established the Robert W. Wilson Galleries in his honor, on the seventh floor of the new building.

Robert Wilson had an association with the American Civil Liberties Union, based in New York City, that was actually slightly longer than his association with the New York Public Library. Wilson was a member of the ACLU for more than forty years. He had become a millionaire in 1966, and by 1972 was worth $21 million, so he was certainly able to, and certainly did, help out financially on a regular basis.

Eventually he became extremely important as a benefactor of the ACLU. Through his charitable trust, established much later, in 2002, he established a "Legacy Challenge," which involved pledging from estate capital, and he was able to direct the grand sum of $200 million-plus (in legacy pledges) to the organization, from thousands of other ACLU members.

All his life, Wilson thought criminal law and criminal punishment in the U.S. needed very serious reforming. He felt that there was terrible injustice here. He was a member of the ACLU, after all, even before the egregious Rockefeller drug laws went into effect in New York state in 1973.

Just Another Sale

"None of us, I suspect, knew…anyone who was as truly, totally, so sui generis as Bob Wilson was."
PAUL LECLERC, PRESIDENT EMERITUS,
THE NEW YORK PUBLIC LIBRARY

The end of Robert Wilson's life, late in 2013, was eerily like the end of his investing career. It was his own decision, it was based on performance issues, it was emphatic and decisive, and it was without a second thought. Wilson had received two signals that the end was nigh. In June, 2013, at home in New York, he had a stroke. Late in November of that same year, he had a more serious one. That was it. The prospects for his mental and physical life were bleak, he knew, and he had no interest in experiencing them. With the grand dispassion that was his hallmark, he ended his life.

Wilson had thrown a big birthday party for himself on November 3, as he always did, at his large apartment in the San Remo building, right across from Central Park. He had turned 87 that day, and he was reported to have been in fine spirits at the party. Very sadly, the happiness did not last long. Several weeks later, he had his second stroke.

He had his affairs well in order. Earlier in 2013 he had said to his friend Stephen Viscusi, "I only have about $100 million to go." He was talking about his net worth, of course. He had gone well past his pledge a dozen years earlier to give away $560 million, or 70% of his wealth. He had given away almost $700 million. In his will he had directed his extensive personal art collection to go to his beloved Whitney Museum of American Art. He had made a number of other gifts in his will, as well. And he had directed that his last remaining estate capital go to—what else—charity. The last $100 million.

On December 23, at home, Wilson sat down at the back of his apartment and wrote a note of farewell. He stated that he had had a good life, a rewarding life, and that he had done everything he wanted to do. He also stated that he felt no shame in doing what he was about to do. As a final practical matter, he set down a short list of upcoming appointments, and noted that they would have to be cancelled. Shortly after the note was finished, the New York City police would find it.

Wilson opened a back window of his apartment, one that looked out onto an inner courtyard. The courtyard was about 150 feet down, and it was empty. There was no one out there; no one down there. Wilson would never have considered a jump from the front side of his apartment, onto busy Central Park West. Absolutely nobody else was going to be harmed by what he was about to do. And there was no harm in him. Never.

Wilson leapt out of the window. It was certainly a frightening few seconds, and without question it was a very brave thing to do. He was killed instantly. America's greatest investor—ever—was gone.

A Note on Sources

Like Shakespeare, Robert W. Wilson left very few traces behind. I am extraordinarily lucky to have known him a bit, after 1989. Wilson had a very active cultural and social life in New York City, and I met him on the social scene.

Fortunately, Wilson was recognized as a world-class investor as early as the late 1960s, and was then followed carefully and in detail, particularly by Barron's weekly financial newspaper, and Forbes magazine, and The Wall Street Journal, and Business Week magazine; and other business publications. Later on, he would appear occasionally in publications concerned with the world of philanthropy.

What I discovered is that the only way to understand the truly extraordinary work and career of Robert Wilson is to work from the outside in. Individual investment after investment, and then philanthropic gift after gift, if these things are studied carefully, and understood in detail, a whole picture of the man behind them begins to emerge. The most important thing about Wilson, and it is not very well known, is that he was every bit as productive as he was talented. He was just tireless, his entire life. He built a great fortune, and then he gave it all away. Along the way, he changed the fortunes of many large and small charities and organizations, and the lives of countless thousands of people, permanently for the good.

Barron's weekly financial newspaper, for many years a great friend of Robert Wilson, once made the comment that Wilson would always reveal to its reporters the common-stock investments he owned, and had sold short, and that it was for him "a congenial chore." In other words, other investors would often read Barron's and then help out Wilson's investment positions, and prices, by piling on.

What Wilson didn't often reveal was exact information, and that is where the Schedule 13D filing comes in, courtesy of the U.S. Securities and Exchange Commission. A Schedule 13D must be filed with the S.E.C. within ten days, by anyone achieving more than a 5% beneficial ownership of any class of stock, in a publicly traded U.S. company. Wilson filed 13Ds all the time, particularly in over-the-counter stocks. It is a small point, but while Wilson would always tell you what he was "long and short," hoping that you'd help him out with your own sympathetic trades, the public 13D filing is the only place where all of the details could be viewed.

During Wilson's investing career (and thereafter), the 13D filing did not apply to individual short positions in a publicly traded stock, larger than 5%. The thinking was that big short-sellers had no interest at all in taking over a business—in fact, just the opposite. Nevertheless, during Wilson's career, for many companies in the U.S., reports of aggregate short positions were required by the S.E.C., and then published on a monthly basis.

About the Author

Roemer McPhee was trained in history at Princeton University, and in finance at the Wharton Graduate School of Business, in Philadelphia. He is the author of *The Boomer's Guide to Story*, a large collection of essays searching for wisdom and insight in modern stories (novels, original screenplays, even a few ballads). He lives in New York City with his wife and son.

Index to Investments Made by Robert Wilson

Robert Wilson Quotes (selected)

"Making money is so much fun."

"You've heard that it's more blessed to give than to receive, but making money is a lot more fun than giving it away."

"Sooner or later, everybody ****s up."

"I wanted to make sure, could I take it with me?" [about his estate planning]

"The bears have nothing left but their telephones!" [start of the 1980s bull market]

"I want my money to do a little bit of good for a lot of people."

"There is incredible psychic pressure in the investing business."

"This business doesn't get to me—not fundamentally."

"I can't stand the New York Times. Oh, there's always somebody suffering somewhere."

"I can't stand the theater."

"On vacation, the only calls I will answer are margin calls."

"To be a short-seller you have to be a masochist, and then try to make money later on."

"You sell a stock short, and then the market keeps pumping up the price after you've sold it."

"I don't know why the press writes all these articles about me."

"The idea that if I don't give some money, something will disappear, that appeals to me."

"You know what a credit balance is, don't you?"

"T. Rowe Price is a big name, but how much *money* does he have? Not all that much!"

"I know a lot of people who have given money away, and usually they've done more harm than good."

"How many hamburgers can America stuff in its face?" [about Wendy's, Inc.]

"If I have to look at another ****ing wildebeest, I'm going to die." [on safari in west Africa]

"I made my big money when I was married."

"The West Side [of New York City] is a great place for a dirty old man."

"I am not going to ride in some limousine. I ride the subway. And it's much faster."

"My goal is to make a billion dollars."

Printed in Great Britain
by Amazon

32174237R00061